Whole Brother

Debunking the Myths That Break the Black Family

Maliek Blade

Copyright © 2020 by **Maliek Blade**

Renown Publishing
www.renownpublishing.com

Whole Brother / Maliek Blade
ISBN-13: 978-1-952602-03-0

This is a book about better.

Oppression does more than simply create an environment in which it is difficult to succeed. It also scars, both emotionally and psychologically. To progress, to overcome, we have to address not only the conditions and structure of such a society, but also the wounds it's inflicted on the body of the people.

In *Whole Brother: Debunking the Myths That Break the Black Family*, Maliek Blade names, claims, and addresses the familial, emotional and physiological issues the Black community deals with every day. He identifies ideas and hurdles that aren't always readily visible and promotes positive change.

To be successful, we must have whole families. To have whole families, we must have whole men. This book is about that. This book is about better.

Judge Lynn Toler, Host of TV's Nationally Syndicated *Divorce Court* and We TV's *Marriage Bootcamp*

I began writing this on my birthday, June 17. I share a birthday with my Uncle Billy. He was with me at the beginning of this writing journey, but he transitioned from this life during the final edits. He was a father, brother, uncle, and friend.

He was my family's personal Richard Pryor and always had a crude but funny joke in his back pocket. Before going on life support, he left us with one last joke. I want him to know that I've laughed more than I've cried, as he would have wanted. I salute him and the following Whole Brothers who—at different times—have played a pivotal role in my development into manhood:

My brother, Jerome Gay Jr.; my godfather, Irvin Belt; my stepfather, Willie Blade; Jay Cameron; Lorenzo Lowery; and William Lee.

CONTENTS

Turning the Tide

I'm often called an old soul or told I'm wise beyond my years. Sure, some might see this as a compliment, and I do appreciate the thought. However, this positive trait comes with the burden of having a different outlook on life than most of my peers. In fact, those who understand me best and share my ideals tend to be much older than I am.

I'd just turned twenty-five as I set out to write this book. My birthday fell on Father's Day, which caused me to reflect on my life. Looking back reminded me of several pivotal moments in my life and the lives of others that were tied to a father's influence or lack thereof. What weighs even more heavily on me is that the norm for us as black men is to live and die without unpacking or understanding how we are personally affected by what our fathers did or did not do.

While the damage caused by absentee fathers is often under-addressed, we tend to completely overlook the fact that fathers who are present sometimes pass on toxic thinking and unhealthy habits. I want to be clear that black men are not the sole bearers of this problem, but the implications in our community are dire. Many of us have accepted unhealthy norms. Societal factors—as well as escapism—play a role in these internal issues persisting.

For example, lifelong friendships are hard to build when most of your peers are solely focused on catching the eye of as many women as possible. This is not just a youthful endeavor. Many adult men share this worldview, and it causes most non-romantic relationships to suffer. Talking about women with your brothers is common, but the vinyl record scratches when a young, black boy has a greater passion than "chasing the cheeks." It all goes back to worldview and who taught whom what is normal and acceptable. For young boys, this is the one area where a father's guidance is needed most.

What happens when a fourteen-year-old boy, much like me when I was in high school, starts thinking about a career that doesn't fit with the culture around him? I remember asking myself, *"Why do other guys only see football, basketball, and rapping as viable careers?"* Why did most of my peers excel in athleticism but fall short of success in areas like public speaking? Who made sports our norm?

In my search for answers, I came to the conclusion that who we are and how we think and act are heavily influenced by who raised us.

I am no stranger to the fact that black men are harshly criticized within our community, but we also face criticism from other communities. With that in mind, I do not want to be another loud voice in a crowd of complainers. I want to be a solution-focused voice with a healthy dose of empathy, as I am a black man myself. This is where I get excited because, while I recognize that I am not the first or only person with answers, I truly believe I am the first to address the specific issue discussed here, in this format, at this phase of life.

I am convinced that black fatherhood and the black family can have a brighter future despite our community dissension. With this book, I will offer a new starting point for us all. I believe a newfound perspective can equip us to weather any storm. Additionally, I will offer some pushback on things we think are okay but really are not okay. I will also issue a challenge for the men.

Is this book that you are holding in your hands a cure-all? Of course not! So, what is it?

This book offers:

- A healthy view of black manhood and masculinity.

- Practical alternatives for unhealthy assumptions that affect interpersonal relationships.

- Insight and hope for those who have a contentious relationship with a black man in their life—be it their father, son, brother, boyfriend, or husband.

Just as black people share a national group identity, we often share the same experiences from north to south and east to west. For example, political pundits often assert that black people should deal with fatherlessness and black-on-black crime within their own communities before being critical of crooked police. In response, I say we can do both simultaneously. The same is true for fatherhood. This book addresses community issues as well as the environment that created them. I believe the things we confess amongst ourselves should not be used to distract from personal issues that we deem important enough to protest or rally around.

A renewed perspective on black male identity is needed not only for black men but also for those who have a vested interest in us, including sons, wives, lovers, and mentors. It is my hope that a son with a strained relationship with his dad will arrive at a newfound perspective of self and that he will be encouraged to reach out. I also hope that he will develop a newfound compassion for his dad, who may not have had the most stable upbringing.

I hope that the wives and others who love black men begin to understand our framework for relationships and the seasons of life we go through. I hope that mentors, pastors, and counselors of black men are invited into an understanding of a narrative that affects how black men receive their guidance.

I hope to put into words what many black men have thought or experienced. After naming the problems, we can deal with them head-on as a community. I believe that dealing with these issues will be the beginning of generational change. One man with a renewed perspective can turn the tide of his family well into the future. One family can turn the tide of a neighborhood. One neighborhood can change a city. And a city can change a nation.

For years, we have been collectively guilty of false practices and ignorance. However, we can be held accountable for what we are made aware of. The black man is not an island. He is not a monolith standing alone. His actions help and hurt those he loves, and the time to change the harmful behaviors of the past is now.

WHOLE BROTHER · 7

CHAPTER ONE

Our False Balance

My mom was 15 and my dad was 16 when my older brother was born. They later married, but they were divorced by the time I was two years old. My father battled—and still battles—a drug addiction, which damaged our relationship and had him in and out of our lives. He had a terrible relationship with his dad, who was never committed to my grandmother—God rest her soul. My mom can count on one hand how many times she has seen her father—God rest his soul. After his death, we discovered he had another family.

When I was a kid, my uncles and older male cousins regularly asked me, "How many girlfriends do you have?" Keep in mind, I was probably eight years old at the time. I was always embarrassed. I had no context for what interaction with females should look like. And sadly, their words set the tone for my future relationships with girls. I began looking at women as something to accumulate, like points or trophies.

Typically, in his early years of life, a boy views everyone as a platonic friend, whether male or female, until that person does something mean. But then puberty kicks in, and women begin to catch his eye. In a perfect world, a dad would have "the talk" with his son and ultimately shape his view of women and how they should be treated.

But what happens when the dad isn't there? Who does this abandoned son learn from? Who will show him balance? Whether intentionally or unintentionally, other men pick up where the dad left off, and what they say and do becomes our norm. A boy learns from the corner boys down the street and the rappers on TV, thereby allowing his impressionable mind to be shaped by those who may not have his best interest in mind.

His transition from boyhood ends up being trial and error rather than him putting his best foot forward with the wisdom of those who came before him. Without guidance, he is left to figure out relationships with women through experimentation. While that may seem normal and acceptable, the downside of it is that the young women who engage with him become casualties of him "figuring it out" because no one taught him the right way. This is the plight of the average young man: trying to balance raging hormones with no context for what healthy relationships should look like.

For example, a young man is likely to have low expectations of relationships and how long they last if his parents are divorced. So, he meets a young woman who wants commitment, and he chooses to move forward with her even if at the time he is playing the field and seeing what else is out there. Why? Once again, if he has not been given a framework for how relationships should be, he is only in it for what he can get out of it. So, he tells her he loves her and sends her good morning text messages—but only if that is what it takes to get what he wants from her. He will also do the same for Jasmine, Brittany, and Shay, because it's really all about getting what he wants.

I'd like to pause for a brief experiment. To the parents reading, I can confidently say that your teen to college-age son is likely in contact with five to ten women at any given time through text and social media. How you verify this is up to you.

Unbalanced behavior from our young men is the result of not being taught self-control and honesty by a father figure. Self-control is how you steward your freedom. Sure, two willing parties may be completely within their rights to sacrifice a relationship and simply have sex. However, parents—specifically fathers—need to do their due diligence in shaping and preparing the minds of their sons before they are presented with such opportunities.

What does an active father figure, whether a biological father or a mentor, teach a young man? A father can impart balance up front before the young man makes mistakes with his relationships and career that he may not be able to repair.

The Father We Need

Pride makes it somewhat impossible to convince an adult man to implement major lifestyle changes, even if there is clear evidence that the current results of his actions are destructive. It's much easier to raise boys than to re-teach grown men. It's a difficult task for one man to gain the trust of another. There is no room to grow when one is disconnected from wise counsel. Father-son relationships as well as mentor-to-mentee dynamics can be established, but they are rare once men pass the age of 30.

Being teachable is challenging because it requires humility. All of us walk around with a level of pride, but, in my experience, it seems black male pride is on steroids. Much of this has to do with the need to appear intimidating so as not to be tested by others on the street or in jail. This is yet another example of society shaping a boy's mind when his father is not there. A father could communicate the balance of being both confident and teachable to his son. As it stands, this lack of teachability makes fathering or any type of guidance from one man to another difficult, if not impossible. We do not like to feel like we are depending on someone else. The problem is that this mindset assumes we can function well while being completely independent of others.

For example, a few years ago, a female friend of mine asked me to help out her troubled brother. She and I had talked about faith and spirituality, her mental illness, and creating healthy relationship patterns. Despite having her own share of personal issues, she allowed her brother to move in with her free of charge. This was meant to be his fresh start, away from his home state.

After he moved in, they began to butt heads about his responsibilities as a guest in her home. She simply asked that he clean up after himself and tidy the shared areas. For whatever reason, he couldn't take care of these very basic chores. This annoyed her, a frustration that was only heightened by the fact that he was nineteen years old. She was justifiably upset with his lack of discipline and respect for others and kicked him out.

Despite not taking care of his responsibilities, he did agree to meet with me per her request. Over the course of nine months, he and I spoke candidly about his past, present, and where he wanted to be in the future. He did not normally have conversations like the kind we had, but his sister's trust in me helped me to earn his trust.

Unfortunately, he fit the all-too-common stereotype for black men.

He aspired to be a successful rapper and intended to take care of his family's needs with his riches. His father was not in his life. His mother introduced him to selling drugs in order to keep the family afloat. He explained that his mom had brought another man around who was beginning to take on a stepfather role, and he welcomed that. Unfortunately, that man later abandoned him as well. Soon, a time came when he and his mother had a falling out, which resulted in him living with his grandmother. Because his grandmother did everything in her house, including his chores, he never developed discipline in those areas because he never had to.

When he began making enough money through selling drugs, he rented an apartment and was then able to make his own rules. His then-girlfriend moved into his apartment, which opened the door for frequent sex. This resulted in his first child, unplanned, at the age of 17. They later broke up due to his infidelity, and the mother was given custody of the child. Due to negligence, she later lost the child, who became the responsibility of the state. A family friend became the child's guardian, and my friend's brother (at the time we were conversing) owed a growing debt in back child support.

Since he was new to the area and had given up selling drugs, I helped him with some basics like finding a job and purchasing health insurance as well as helping him develop a plan to reach his long-term goal of regaining custody of his daughter. As we talked, he came to the realization that he did not see being a part of his daughter's life as urgent because he was still trying to enjoy his youth. I shared the potential implications of his absence on his daughter, connecting his actions to how he felt about the absence of his own father, coupled with the rejection of his stepfather-to-be.

In our conversation about health insurance, we naturally progressed to the potential results of a reckless sex life. When he shared about his relational patterns and the number of partners he'd had, I encouraged him to get tested for sexually transmitted diseases. After finding a doctor that would accommodate him in his current financial state, we set up an appointment for a general physical and STD testing. He learned he had herpes simplex virus 2, which is incurable. He had a three-year-old daughter in a different state, back child support, and an STD. He was not on speaking terms with his child's mother, he had no license or car, and he had no place to stay because his sister kicked him out due to disrespect.

In addition to his chaotic lifestyle, I noticed erratic emotional extremes. One day he was excited about taking steps to get established as an independent man, and then the next he wanted to remain in isolation and ignored everyone's text messages. It was later revealed that he did indeed suffer from bipolar disorder. In his case, he did not like the way the medication made him feel, so when he began living on his own, he refused to take it. As a result, his condition grew worse.

Sustaining relationships became hard. The twisted conclusions he drew from conversations caused him to act out against other parties, thus pushing them away. I observed him long enough to change my position on him having custody of his daughter. In my personal opinion, he was a danger to himself and not fit to raise a child. His presence in his daughter's life would have been toxic, but his absence was damaging as well.

To ask whether we should be present in a child's life demands that we take a good, hard look at ourselves. This young man did not have the best start in life. His father was absent, and his mother was toxic. As I spoke with him, I did not lay blame on him for his unfortunate situation. He was not given proper guidance as a child, and his life became experimentation without preparation.

Is this young man's story too outrageous to believe? Unfortunately, it is far too common for many black boys and men.

Yes, we learn from our mistakes. But sometimes mistakes have consequences that cannot be reversed. It is much safer to learn from the wisdom of a father and avoid those costly mistakes entirely. This young man saw the need for a remedy in his family's unhealthy behavioral cycle, but he thought it would come from a successful rap career and money. I explained that these cycles would persist regardless of how much money he made because these issues were not there solely because of a lack of resources. He needed balance.

His dream of a having a healthy family had to start with him becoming a physically, emotionally, and spiritually healthy individual. Note: the emphasis is on health, not perfection.

Because I came along later in his life and he'd experienced so many hurts in his past, the young man had difficulty taking my advice and felt trapped in a cycle of bad habits. What he didn't understand is that none of us are all-knowing. We need the experiences and knowledge of others because we only know what we know. Our genius is limited to our experiences and how much we're willing to listen. Unfortunately, many of us would rather do things our way first, fail, and then perhaps listen to what others have to say because we want to be independent. This is a waste of time.

For this reason, I am advocating for fathers to take their roles seriously when their children are young. Get help with personal development and set the tone for a new way of living for future generations. I believe the solution for the anonymous gentleman mentioned, other men, and me is an intact home rather than a broken one. When that is not possible, we must seek to find a father figure who can be trusted. Bravado says, "I have it all under control," while reality is saying, "This ain't it, bro."

My Experience

The pattern is clear: many men make children easily enough but never seem to get around to establishing homes. I do not believe that men in these cycles are simply bad people. I believe that many of us do not know what we are doing. We have not been taught. In addition to not knowing how to balance our lives, life does not slow down to accommodate a learning curve, and we almost never get a redo. This is why black men must be taught to understand the weight of their responsibility—so they can break the cycle.

Before attaching ourselves to a woman or bringing a child into the world, we should take the time to develop ourselves and ensure we are adding to the lives of others instead of just taking for ourselves. We have reached a cultural moment where sex is no longer a sacred act within a covenant relationship. It is now simply seen as a mutually beneficial favor amongst acquaintances. Now that sex is easily had, so are children. It's time to face the music.

Oftentimes, we as men are simply seeking a sexual release without the strings of commitment and responsibility. As a result, when one of the many women a guy is sleeping with ends up pregnant, it's more of an inconvenience than a joyous celebration of life. In effect, we are making accidental families with women we did not necessarily intend to build a home with. When acquaintances have sex and then later realize they cannot stay together after having a child, the child suffers. Brothers, we must do better—not just for ourselves but for the children we create, who did not ask to be here.

What Do I Do Now?

The process begins with asking the questions: What about me is broken? And how do I fix it?

I had to answer those questions for myself. My mother did not do baby talk. She always spoke to me as though I was a young man. This caused me to communicate like an adult very early in life. I also read through the entire dictionary when I was eleven years old. I believe these factors contributed to why, upon meeting me as a child, many people thought I was smart.

Of course, speaking well does not necessarily mean having a vast amount of knowledge. The compliments and approval from adults went to my head, and I developed an ego at a very young age. I don't think arrogance is a strong enough word to describe what I was giving off to others. I managed to have a good image while being very hypocritical at times. This may seem like a minor issue, but my grade-school teachers would disagree.

When I was in sixth grade, my teacher explained that some of the issues I was having with my classmates were due to me being more mature than they were, and that I would find more camaraderie in high school and college—as those who were immature and lacking discipline would be weeded out. While this may have been true, I was not mature enough to process the explanation in a healthy way. I was on my way to being well known but not well liked.

What helped me achieve some level of balance to find success? I found men I respected for their minds and balanced lifestyles, and I had frank conversations with them. I asked them to be honest, and they shared some hard truths with me. "You lack compassion," they told me, and "Yes, you're smart, but it does not matter if everybody hates you."

Balance in Brokenness

Often, we can trace a life that lost balance and went downhill back to an unresolved childhood issue. Although a son and father may be a victim and a perpetrator respectively, it is possible for both of them to live their lives without ever knowing it.

In many ways, the future of a young boy is in the hands of his father. What the father does or does not do often has a direct impact on how the son turns out. We need black fathers to lead the way in reconciling broken black families.

Being a man doesn't mean we instinctively know how to be a good father. If you're broken, choose to stop the cycle. Find the help you need; then help the children you have created to find the balance they so desperately need.

Humble yourself by accepting that you need help. If you find yourself repeating the same cycles, then you do not have everything under control.

Reach out to one trustworthy and stable man for guidance and actually listen to him. This man may be a mentor, pastor, or therapist. From there, seek out additional men to invest in you. Their wealth of knowledge will make you a better man.

Take fatherhood seriously. Do not create another life if you can barely manage your own.

Work toward viewing women as people, not prizes. You cannot be woke with a trail of broken black women behind you.

In terms of life progression, follow this order of development: Me (self-development) > Her (relationship development) > Them (family development). Don't be so quick to jump from Me to Her.

CHAPTER TWO

Four Types of Fathers

In today's world, where gender roles in the home are fluid, co-parenting for divorced couples has been normalized, and single parents are idealized, I hold to the traditional view. A child needs a mother *and* a father who are emotionally and mentally healthy and who are both dedicated to raising their children.

The key ingredient to the mixture that is often left out today is the father.

A father creates a safe space in our world for a family to grow. Not only is he a protector, an engaged father's presence shapes the character of his children, especially his son(s). While mothers have an influential role as well, a father's actions set the tone for what is normal and acceptable in romantic relationships. While this does not guarantee that the son will never have problems, a faithful father will fill many of the voids within young men that lead to them seeking identity validation through women.

Unfortunately, homes are too often burdened with an absent or distant father, a mother forced to act as father, or a toxic father, each creating an unhealthy environment that plagues the family from generation to generation. Let us take a closer look at each of these four types of fathers, what these men do, and how the cycle of bad parenting can be broken.

The Absent Father

As I think back on my male friends and schoolmates during my younger years, I can count on one hand how many lived in households with their dad. Many lived with their mom solely, but an even larger number lived with their grandmother.

An absent father is a father who lives outside of the home where his son lives and is not involved in his son's life. This is an unfortunate occurrence for many black children.

One of the most popular episodes of *The Fresh Prince of Bel-Air* is episode 24 of the fourth season. Although it originally aired in 1994, a specific clip from that episode is still regularly shared on social media. If you are not familiar with *The Fresh Prince of Bel-Air*, I have no words for you besides "Do your Googles."

Will, the protagonist of *The Fresh Prince of Bel-Air*, had an absent father. When speaking to his uncle, Will responded to his father's leaving again by trying to act strong and saying he didn't need his father since he had been absent for fourteen years while Will was growing up. Will lists various childhood and teenage milestones he managed to accomplish without his father's presence before angrily vowing to succeed in life:[1]

Hey, he wasn't there to teach me how to shoot my first basket, but I learned, didn't I? ... Got through my first date without him, right? I learned how to drive, I learned how to shave, I learned how to fight without him. ... I'ma get through college without him, I'ma get a great job without him, I'ma marry me a beautiful honey, and I'ma have me a whole bunch of kids. I'll be a better father than he ever was.

After his outburst, Will falls into his Uncle Phil's arms, sobbing, saying, "How come he don't want me, man?"

It might be as loud as a passing fire truck or as quiet as a whisper, but Will's question, "How come he don't want me, man?" resounds in the heads of sons who have been deserted by their father. And in most cases, there's no Uncle Phil in their lives to give guidance or direction.

I've learned not to take my own father's absence personally. He struggles with a drug addiction, which means he is constantly in and out of rehabilitation centers. He is currently not able to establish consistency for the sake of his own well-being, so I understand why he is unable to be involved in my life. But what about the fathers who are fully and physically able to be part of their sons' lives but choose not to? It hurts the son all the more.

A young man may not know that he is hurt, but the pain manifests itself in a variety of ways.

The First Consequence: Spiteful Success

Spiteful success is when a son parades his accomplishments before others to prove his worth. In practice, this is an abandoned son acknowledging his father's departure, then deciding to pursue excellence not for personal conviction or to care for a family but to prove to himself or his father that he is worthy of love and worthy of a relationship and honest communication. The lie the son accepts is that because his father left, the son is not desirable or worthy of relationship. In response, he goes above and beyond in everything to prove himself worthy.

In part, a boy's identity is formed through affirmation from his parents, especially his father. This means that regardless of what negativity he hears from the broader culture, he is anchored in positive feedback and support at home.

However, when affirmation does not happen at home, he seeks identity and affirmation from the broader culture—the huge cultural pool that is the world. In a search for belonging, the trend is for a young black man to find himself in street gangs, sports teams, frats, and the like. Essentially, it is a personal attempt at creating a solid family unit.

This issue manifests itself differently based on geography and socioeconomic status. Some men spend a lifetime trying to fit in somewhere because they didn't receive affirmation at home during their developmental years. When the foremost person in a man's life—his father—is not present, the man ends up broken because he is missing half of the primary contribution to his development. The other half of the contribution comes from his mother. Although some downplay the lack of relationship with their father, I would argue it is a recurring thought and a painful memory that often causes young men to try to prove their worth.

Success itself isn't bad, but using success to spite his father can ultimately bring more frustration. Whether it is being drafted in the NBA or some other major accomplishment, there is no guarantee that the absent father will then be impressed or interested in a relationship.

The Second Consequence: Lens of Abandonment

A lens is the way a person looks at the world. Think of it like a pair of glasses. When you look through sunglasses, the world changes and looks much dimmer.

For example, a religious person will see God in everything and expect God to be a part of the world. Someone who loves sports will see the world as a competition where someone wins and someone loses.

The child who has been abandoned by his father will naturally see the world through the lens of abandonment.

This lens has drastic consequences. The young man's father abandoned him. Now who will be the next to leave? His mother? Girlfriend? Friends? Coach? Teacher? If his father has left him, he'll approach the next relationship with the immanent fear that the person is about to leave at any moment. If it's easy for one of the most important people in his life to leave him, how much easier will it be for someone who is less connected to him?

This unhealthy expectation throws a negative layer of assumption on to otherwise potentially well-meaning people. A non-invite or exclusion will be interpreted as a malicious act or a sign that the relationship is on the way out.

The lens of abandonment strains relationships by imposing the fear of the wounded on the innocent. It is a form of self-sabotage that creates a toxic situation for others, and many times a young man will try to stay one step ahead of being abandoned by being the one who leaves first.

He will need endless assurance in each relationship he builds that his friend or partner will not abandon him. Because this isn't a one-time request for a guarantee of acceptance and permanence, the other person finds themselves in a frustrating cycle of constantly having to prove that they are loyal.

The Third Consequence: Codependence

Lessons taught by a father include simple tasks such as how to work, how to groom, and how to communicate. Romantic relationships, jobs, and friendships require work and commitment from both parties. The son who has no father to train him in how to build those relationships and networks will find himself falling behind those who do have training. He ends up being the needy one in most, if not all, of his relationships, both platonic and romantic.

The codependent son is needy with his friends and in his romantic relationships. With his friends, he is playing catch-up. Friends have to teach or help him with basic things like hygiene, money management, and time management. These are areas in which his father should have instructed him. Because his father was absent, this guy will lag behind. He may be the only one in his friend group without a car or degree.

In his romantic relationships, his woman ends up being a mother. She has to tend to his emotional immaturity and communication issues. The situation mirrors the mishaps previously mentioned with his friendships, but there is the added element of his need to be constantly reaffirmed by her. This young man may be described as an overly emotional or weak man. Let me be clear—there's nothing wrong with finding affirmation from relationships. Toxicity enters the relationship when a man expects his girlfriend to fill a void no one can fill, the void from his father leaving.

If you see yourself in this section, that is a good thing and not a bad thing. Now that you realize you are doing these things, you can take steps to change. Although possible, it is extremely difficult to undo these habits independently. I always recommend processing through things in trusted community. When you do not have a father, look for the next best thing to help you get the wisdom and support you need. Find a trusted mentor to support you on your journey.

Present-but-Distant Father

I have a friend who is now in the NBA. We were friends as kids, and he had a dream of going pro. He worked hard to get there, and his father was a big supporter. His father coached him, took him to AAU camps, and overall prepared him to be a college athlete and later a professional athlete.

But my friend once told me that the only thing his dad talked to him about was basketball. That was their only common interest. His dad never got to know him personally, never talked about feelings, never talked about things that made him happy or sad outside of basketball. They never talked about dating or relationships. He described it as being a business relationship.

His dad was only invested in developing him as an athlete. While there isn't anything wrong with enjoying one aspect of a relationship, it falls short of what a son needs for emotional development. When there is no communication surrounding emotion, there is no education regarding emotion. The son will learn from other people and sources.

The present-but-distant father thinks he's doing a great job because he is physically present—either by living in the same house or by being present in his children's lives for specific occasions—but he doesn't consider the implications of his lack of emotional connection. His relationship with his children revolves around common interests like sports and hobbies, but he never takes the time to get to know his children on a personal level.

Many times, we perceive the purpose of manhood or fatherhood as simply to protect and provide food and shelter. In that sense, the bar is set very low because that's what beavers do. The beaver builds a dam for its family and brings them food. Raise the bar for manhood! In addition to providing food and shelter, we need to be emotional supporters, spiritual guides and mentors, and friends. A personal connection is needed.

Being a fully present father is difficult for someone who didn't have a deep relationship with his own father.

A distant father may be distant not because of an issue with his children but because he can only do what he has seen and teach what he knows. He may not know any other way. The son then looks elsewhere for fulfillment of his emotional needs.

Often, when a son is emotionally confused and needs advice, he ends up suppressing his feelings or possibly venting his emotions to his mom. Because sons and daughters turn to Mom with feelings, Dad becomes even more emotionally distant. As a result, Dad becomes a tool that is used as a means to an end. Kids need money to buy a car, Dad buys a car. Kids need clothes, Dad sends money. He works hard to get the kids in sports camps. School activities cost money. Dad becomes a tool while Mom becomes the person who is contributing toward the kids' personal development. The cycle solidifies these roles.

The son of a present-but-distant father is only used to a female response to his emotions, creating an unbalanced emotional life. Because he hasn't had a masculine response to his emotions and because he's only been venting his frustrations to his mom—or worse, bottling them up—he has no idea how to respond healthily when he is hurting or feeling lost and Mom is not around.

He typically has authority issues because he isn't used to a man speaking with power or with firm direction. Because he's been emotionally trained by his mother, he may be crushed or become angry and belligerent when society doesn't give him the response his mom was able to give him. How Mom brings truth may look much different from how Dad brings truth, and both are needed. Loss of one causes the son to miss out and creates a level of imbalance in his life.

This distance that is felt is not due to location but to communication. How and what we communicate will determine the depth of the relationship. Dr. Timothy

Muehlhoff and Bryan Loritts popularized the Communication Pyramid, which assists in building relationships that go beyond the surface.[2] It's a joy to be fully known by someone without having to hide certain aspects of yourself. Below is my spin on this helpful tool:

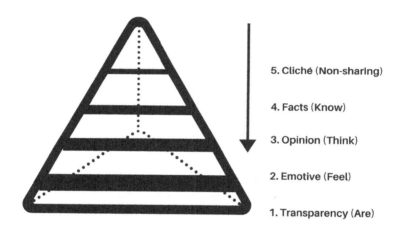

5. Cliché (Non-sharing)

4. Facts (Know)

3. Opinion (Think)

2. Emotive (Feel)

1. Transparency (Are)

The son who has been raised by a present-but-distant father may mirror his dad's distant approach in how he relates to people. He has built a wall to hide behind, and he doesn't understand how to be fully transparent with who he is. The chasm of distance widens when he has negative experiences with people, such as betrayals or relationships that simply do not work out. This is then used as justification to not trust people and maintain a distance. Don't trust everybody but also don't trust nobody.

The communication pyramid explains some of the differences between the different layers of communication. There are five different layers from top to bottom.

The top level of communication is five—clichés. Communication is cliché when it remains at the surface level and is non-sharing. For example, one may say, "Wassup?" Some may say, "How you feelin'?" Guys are famous for saying, "I'm good," even if all hell is breaking loose in their lives. They're just throwing out clichés that we all use to get the conversation over with so we can go about our day. Many times, busy people or introverts resort to clichés because they don't want to engage in certain conversations. These platitudes are nice things we all say, but they really don't mean much.

Communication with a present-but-distant father can often remain here. The son is simply another acquaintance, another person the father might work with or pass on the street.

Level four is facts. This is what you know. This level of communication is sharing what you know, what happened, what you saw, and what was said. This is simply sharing about an accident that happened on the highway or the Patriots winning the Super Bowl. These are all facts we are sharing with each other, so we are just exchanging information.

Pure data passed on to a son is not enough to help him become the man he needs to be. It also only accounts for part of what is needed to take on the responsibility of caring for a family. Transferring facts offers possible information to live a healthy life, but it is a starting point, not the ending point.

Level three is offering opinions. For example, I might say, "A tornado is coming." But all I'm relaying is a fact. If I say, "Since the tornado is coming, I think it's best to stock up on water and bread," then I just gave an opinion, or my personal thoughts based on the factual information.

This is the first layer where communication is personal. It goes beyond information sharing, and we get to the uniqueness of what is going on in your head. It is what you think about any given thing. Sharing what you think about facts might seem like a strong step, but it still lacks the power of breaking down walls and going deep. Let's not forget, we're talking about dynamics between a father and son. If this relationship isn't fully transparent, then where else can you go to be real?

Level two is emotion. This is when you share what you feel about something. You don't just communicate what you think about a situation, but express emotions about what is about to happen, or talk about how something made you feel. "I'm worried that the tornado will leave us displaced."

Sharing your feelings—I'm upset, I'm happy, I'm scared, I'm nervous—creates a sense of openness in a relationship. Fathers that have learned to process through their emotions in a healthy way will raise their children to express their emotions and communicate how they feel. This setting normalizes emotion for boys who, if they are growing up in the hood, are likely to suppress feelings and say less, not more. However, to be the father you're supposed to be, there's another level of communication you need to attain.

Level one is transparency, which means sharing who you are. This takes extra work because you first have to know who you are.

Most men hang out at level five and level four. Even at the deepest level of friendship, where someone says, "This is my best friend, this is my brother," the relationship probably consists of conversations that are limited to clichés and facts. If these men are lucky, they reach level three, where they can freely express an opinion. When a man gets into a relationship with a woman, she may be coming in at level two or level one. He may not know how to respond to such transparent communication. He may not communicate at that level because he has never done so before; he hasn't been taught, because his father didn't demonstrate it. His father was present-but distant.

A better way to explain this is the racial divide in our country. In the news, we hear that an unarmed black man was shot by the police. Many times, we go to social media to air our justified frustrations. African Americans are expressing their concerns around this event at level three all the way down to level one. Sometimes my white brothers and sisters will also engage with the issue on social media, but they are coming in at level five or four. We are missing each other. We're not coming at the conversation at the same level of contribution or with the same goals. Someone communicating at level four has a goal of clarifying the facts, but that may come off as offensive to someone who is expressing their raw feelings at level two. One is not necessarily wrong or right. The appropriateness of a response depends on the type of relationship and the subject. Men need training on how to speak at level one and two with each other.

The relationship with the present-but-distant father is all wrapped together within this communication pyramid. The flaw lies in the inability to communicate at the deepest levels. Sincere, transparent communication is taught by a father leading by example, by practicing with a son, and by sharing deeply his secret desires, hopes, dreams, emotions, and needs. Detached children are typically the result of a detached parent. When that is not the case, a son may be detached from his parents because he has gotten used to only communicating with them at level five and four. He then finds comfort in sharing at level three on down with his perceived friends. Once this divide has been created in the son's head, it's hard to go back and create an atmosphere of transparency between father and son. It's on the dad to set the tone correctly.

Mother as a Father

The third type of "father" is a mother acting as a father. This is a single mother who is, for whatever reason, no longer in any contact with the father of her children and raising her son by herself. She typically has a hard time raising a boy on her own.

She is often overwhelmed by having to play the role of a mother *and* a father. This dual role is outside of the natural design. She is only meant to play the role of the mother, a duty that, in itself, is difficult even at the best of times. When the father is absent, she is forced to carry an overwhelming weight, which is not fair to her or to her children.

Because the father is gone, some mothers feel the need to overcompensate, setting aside their own skills and gifts. They overcorrect for not being a man, but they misunderstand manhood as aggressiveness. They're overly antagonistic with their son in order to keep him from being soft, not realizing that they are hurting their son more than helping him.

Once again, these mothers shouldn't have to take on the father role anyway. If a mother compensates for the lack of masculinity in the home by acting in what she perceives to be masculine ways, it deprives the son of the feminine presence in his life and confuses him as he looks for his masculine identity. The son feels like a failure when his mom is constantly correcting him and never pleased with him. It is neither the mother's nor the son's fault—they are simply in a less than ideal home dynamic.

The second approach a mother playing a father can take is the coddling mom. This approach is what makes the "momma's boys." The mother recognizes that she can't be a father, so even though she has to fill that role, she shrinks back to her gut reaction, which is to be a nurturer, protector, and emotional supporter.

This kind of mother pampers her son and never calls him out when he's wrong. She doesn't challenge him to become a better person. She just affirms and supports him regardless of the circumstance. Although her intent is to give her son more love to make up for the lack of a father, she ends up being the biggest yes-man in his corner, and she is ultimately an enabler, to his detriment.

The issue here is that the son never understands independence because his mom clings tighter in moments when she should let go and allow her son to feel the weight of his decisions.

Consequences of the Mother as a Father Role

There are two common character flaws that appear in the son when a mother plays the father.

First, the son becomes the mother's shadow instead of spreading his wings. He adopts many, if not all, of her personality traits, good or bad. If she is quick to anger, then the son will be the same way. While the anger of a single mother is often easily understood, the anger of a black man is often seen as a threat.

The son who has become another version of his mother has to recognize that he cannot move within the world like his mother without being perceived in a much different way than she is because he is a man. Societally, it is not normal for men to express hurt or offense. Conversely, we tend to expect that from women.

A son raised by an expressive mom may take the expressive approach in his relationships and be perceived as feminine or weak, especially if he raises concerns to male peers. Unfortunately, we typically only allow men to express anger or frustration, even though in reality they have just as extensive an emotional spectrum. A father could help bring the balance of acknowledging emotion while approaching peers in an appropriate manner.

The second character flaw is that the son becomes the mother's enemy. Mother and son may find themselves constantly at odds with each other due to met or unmet expectations. While the mom may project the father's negative character traits onto the son, the son sees the mom's shortcomings in her attempt to be a father as well.

This all ties back to the missing piece—the father. If the father was a cheater, liar, or whatever the case may be, the mom perceives the same tendency in the son. Meanwhile, the son, although his mother is already overwhelmed, is holding her to an unrealistic standard and expects her to fill the role of his father.

When a mother has to take on the father role, mother and son are constantly at odds with each other. Their relationship is strained because the family's foundation has taken a hit due to Dad's absence. They don't understand each other. There is no mediator. A mother acting as father not only deprives her son of a true male role model but also of a true mother, as she feels forced to step out of her lane. Ultimately, both mother and son suffer tremendously in this situation, seeing each other through the lens of the dad who is not present.

Toxic Father

The toxic father is the father who is present, but because he has not developed as an individual, brings negative, improper, unjust, and problematic habits, behaviors, and thought processes into the household. He pollutes the children and mom. In fact, most of the people he comes into contact with are negatively influenced. The home, however, is the place most affected.

The toxic father doesn't realize he is toxic. His norms are his norms, yet those "norms" are upsetting the entire family. Often, it's not until the relationship has broken between him and the mother, or after the children leave the household, that he sees that his actions are not acceptable. However, as long as his children are under his roof, he sets the culture for the home.

My father's drug addiction is an excellent example of this. He would have been a toxic influence for me if I had been around him more. He would frequently sell our property to strangers in exchange for drugs and then disappear. There was no communication. My mom was forced to take every initiative to shield me from him.

Because he was toxic, it was best that he was not directly involved in my life. I understand this to be a point of contention, as it is problematic when women keep their kids from the father for petty reasons. I firmly stand against that. Being a toxic father, however, isn't a petty reason, and it necessitates separation or moderated communication.

Don't get me wrong, I am a champion of fathers being in their children's lives. We know the unfortunate stories of a mom, in bitterness, keeping children from their father just because she's upset that the relationship didn't work. I am not an advocate of that kind of separation. Issues can be talked through.

However, there is a point where a father is so toxic that he shouldn't be around his children. If a father is involved in gangs, in the drug game, or regularly strapped (carrying guns), staying with him may not be best because he may be a target, thus putting the children in mortal danger.

There are several other areas that would make a father toxic enough to the point that he shouldn't be around his kids:

- He is a danger to them. For example, he may be a physical danger to them because people are after the father. Those people may be trying to hurt him, and they may hurt the children instead.

- He has a mental illness. While not all mental illnesses require a father to be separated from his children, some mental illnesses may make him a danger to others.

- He is sexually or physically abusive to his children, wife, or others.

- He is verbally or emotionally abusive. Discipline is one thing, but putting your kids down with your words is another.

- He is immoral. We all have different ideas of what is good and bad, and that is why it's very important to be selective about who you choose to have children with. A father with a fallen morality presents bad things to the child as good things, such as selling drugs, using drugs, excessive drinking, and manipulating people for personal gain.

Sometimes a father's absence is better than his unhealthy presence. That is essentially what's going on with a toxic father—although he is present, his presence is felt in a bad way. He is present but not leading well. Think of some of the people you dislike the most. I'm talking about the people you hope will not be mentioned when you ask, "Who all gonna be there?" People who have that negative effect on the masses typically are damaged, likely by the presence of a toxic father in their lives.

The Consequences of a Toxic Father

The character flaw of the son who has a toxic father is that he adopts the father's character flaws, thus becoming his shadow. If the father is physically abusive to women, then the son is physically abusive in relationships as well.

He mirrors the things his dad does. This father and son duo are on the same page personally, but they are both negative presences in the lives of others.

Even if the son realizes that his father is toxic and doesn't want to be like him, the son unfortunately mirrors him anyway. For some reason, as men we often find it easy to make company with other men who we know have bad character. These are learned behaviors. We may not realize it's happening, but we exhibit what we've observed. We cannot demonstrate something we have not learned. Over time, when the son leaves home, the son imitates his father's character flaws and is equally as damaging to those with whom he comes into contact, creating a cycle. This flaw is rooted in the power of a father's influence. The son may question his father's actions in his mind, but the resolution ends up being, *"If it is okay for my dad, then it must be okay for me."*

These unhealthy habits will create deep relational damage even before the son becomes a father. A toxic father produces a toxic son who is a toxic friend or toxic boyfriend as well, normalizing unhealthy things and bringing that baggage into new relationships.

A second character flaw is being the father's enemy. The son is constantly at odds with the dad. He sees inadequacies because his dad doesn't have good qualities like his mother. Of course, if the son isn't in good standing with the mom, then he is at odds with both parents. This comes through differences in how the son perceives the parents' actions and ultimately depends on who the son gravitates toward more. If the son gravitates more toward the father, then he is likely going to be his father's shadow. If he gravitates more toward the mother, then he is more likely to become his father's enemy. This son judges his dad based on how he compares to his mom, just like the son of a mother as a father judges his mom based on how she compares to his dad.

The third character flaw is the hybrid. The son exhibits the father's characteristics although they are at odds. The son seeks to avoid the mistakes his father makes, but he hasn't been trained on how to overcome the bad habits. All he knows is what he has seen. Even though he recognizes that his father's abuses are wrong, he ends up repeating them because he hasn't been taught otherwise. In times of crisis or uncertainty, we resort to what's most familiar. In this case, the son knows the unhealthy approach that his father takes, and the son resorts to that because it's his norm, whether he means to or not.

These flaws create relational patterns when the son adopts the father's approach to relationships. What happens if the son has a toxic father who is self-centered in relationships? When the son connects with women, he's typically doing so with a self-centered purpose. The son is using women for his benefit, whether it be for affirmation, for sex, or for a place to stay if he is struggling financially. He brings into those relationships whatever character flaws the dad has. He is continuing the cycle of abuse and unhealthiness because, once again, he is adopting what the father did. He is taking bad habits to a new space, and this can play out many unfortunate ways. The uniqueness here is that the son doesn't realize he is doing this. His intentions are not to be like his father, but his practice unintentionally mirrors his father. Many men can relate to unintentionally becoming the thing we hate.

If said son connects to a passive woman who had a toxic father, she may accept the abuse or unhealthy behavior because she may think of this as the norm. She may think that it's just life. Or if she pushes back on him, there will be a rift between the two. How did the son's father deal with pushback from his wife? If the father abused the mother, the son will in turn deal with the pushback in the same way.

Friendships also become relational access to personal

gain without investing in others. So, going back to the communication pyramid, this son stays at level five and four with his friends, which is just enough to get by and to get what he needs from people. He may connect with certain people because it gives him stature and makes him look important, valuable, and more popular. He connects with people not for the actual benefit and pleasure of friendship but for personal gain, personal advancement, or personal goals. It's transactional. For others, it is impossible to connect with him on a personal level because, once again, he sees people as a means to accomplish his purposes.

Toxic people are often toxic because they only consider themselves and what benefits them. A toxic person damages other people intentionally or unintentionally because he is only thinking about himself. When that person is a father, he will likely pass on his toxic traits to his male children. Therefore, in the case of a toxic father, a mother may be wise to keep her children away from him to protect them from being abused and, eventually, negatively influenced by their father. A toxic father is a terrible example of manhood and fatherhood, and his influence is deeply negative and should be avoided if at all possible.

CHAPTER THREE

Myth #1—Men Walk Alone

A friend of mine describes himself as an extreme introvert, a lone wolf, and extremely non-social. He considers himself a man who walks alone.

I do not deny that some guys are introverts and others prefer not to socialize frequently. These are neutral parts of someone's personality. However, we often label something a personality trait when it is actually a response to trauma or a coping mechanism. Sometimes we are not able to tell the difference between introversion and social isolation due to depression. There is a tendency to expect women to be social butterflies with large friend groups, and the opposite is expected of men. Both women and men believe that part of being a man is being alone. When this happens, that second look we would give an isolated woman is not extended to men, and the question isn't asked, "Are you okay?"

Many men believe that being a man means being the silent hero, suffering alone, and giving of self until there isn't anything left to give. While we like to portray ourselves as all powerful superheroes, the reality is that we are all mortal men with mental and physical limitations. We must accept that it's okay to ask for help and that it does not make us any less masculine. As men, sometimes we need help. We do not have all the answers. We were made for community; no man in complete isolation is thriving. As the English poet John Donne wrote, "No man is an island entire of itself; every man is a piece of the continent, a part of the main."[3]

Walking alone is simply an improper response to stimuli. It is a false attempt at self-protection. Most often, it can be tied to a series of negative experiences with people that have not been resolved. The internal resolution is, *"I can avoid these negative experiences by removing myself."* It may provide some relief, but it is self-damaging as well. If someone withdraws every time something goes wrong, they will end up alone most of the time because life is not "positive vibes only."

Additionally, some men have the mindset that it's best not to relate to friends, their mom, their father, or their siblings because they're afraid of not meeting their expectations. Some men disappear because they do not feel personally adequate to meet the expectations of their loved ones. The solution is to isolate themselves because they believe that without a connection, they won't disappoint.

What they miss is that this isolation grieves the loved ones who are seeking to connect with them. Guys typically do not verbalize it this way, but it is how they rationalize and deal with difficult relationships, offenses, and rough patches. This plays out in different ways.

For example, a man who is a lone wolf will sometimes become offended by a friend's actions and refuse to work through the offense or explain what was done to offend him. He just gets offended and isolates himself. He rarely allows his relationships to get to a deeper level.

If this guy chooses to make friends, those relationships will likely consist of level five and four conversations exclusively because he knows it's safe and there are limited expectations. While it may sound backwards, men who are walking alone often desire and need community and communication. Their fear of neglect, betrayal, or being a disappointment cripples them and keeps them in a very unhealthy space. An isolated man is missing out on what others have to offer, and others are missing out on what he brings to the table.

One cannot learn without being connected to a source of knowledge. One cannot be encouraged if one is disconnected from encouragers. Oftentimes, depression is diagnosed by a professional when others point out a pattern. Lastly, disregarding what others can contribute, a man cannot leave a legacy by which to be remembered without investing in others.

A man who avoids isolation and walks with others is able to sense the needs of others and support loved ones in difficult times. I can be a better son to my mom by being available and understanding about some of the things that she went through.

I have one biological brother, and he is the oldest. At one point, my mom was carrying twins, who were supposed to be born between my brother and me. We lost the twins. One died very early on in my mother's pregnancy, and the other twin, whose name would have been Jordan, was born dead.

Every year around the time when Jordan would have been born, my mom gets sad. Even though more than twenty-six years have passed, she gets into a dark place around that time. Some years are better than others, but she remembers the pain of losing her children. Since I've taken the time to invest in her, I have stayed interested and connected to her even in my adult years. I am able to support her just by reaching out or listening if she reaches out. She knows I'm on her side.

Of course, her husband should be her ultimate supporter, but her sons are able to come alongside her as well, if we aren't consumed with our world or disconnected from everyone.

These aspects of learning who people are helps us to serve them better. If we are disconnected, we don't get the opportunity to learn about who they are. When we isolate ourselves, we miss out on the opportunity to give back to those who poured into us in our developmental years.

The implication for men who walk alone is a symptom they may not recognize—they only focus on themselves. If this is true, help is needed. Although it is my life, it is not all about me. Isolated men are only doing what's most convenient for them. Sometimes this is selfishness, and other times it's something deeper. Those who isolate themselves are not always the bad guys. Oftentimes, there's a series of events that got them to that point.

The Better Way: An Alternative

The friend I mentioned at the beginning of the chapter was a lone wolf. He and I had a falling out when we were teens. We've reconnected now, but from our teen years until recently, I didn't see much positive change in him. I believe he didn't mature because he was disconnected from people.

I must admit, I've not been the model friend to him. I've sought help, gone to therapy, and talked through issues he and I have. I've spoken to my parents about issues, and I have talked to his parents as well. I've invested time, and now we are in a better, although not ideal, place. I have grown, and both he and I have made apologies. I have taken responsibility for the ways I failed to communicate properly and the negativity I brought to the friendship when we were teens.

Now that we are full-grown adults, I was prepared to do things in an adult way, having matured and moved forward. However, when I first reconnected with him in our adult years, I discovered he was still offended from when we were fifteen because he hadn't taken the time to process through the hurt and difficulties that we went through with other people. Rather than processing through conflict in community with others, he isolated himself and tried to block things out. His process was to isolate himself until he felt better about the situation and then reconnect as if the offense never happened. When you isolate yourself, you miss out on the insight and wisdom of others and potentially stunt your own growth.

My friend had bottled up his emotions, so when I was talking to him all these years later, he was still in the same spot because he was embracing the idea that men walk alone and that's just the way it is. He assumed—and a lot of men assume—that he was all-sufficient and any issue that he had he could solve by himself. That idea is simply not true. No one is all-knowing. No one has all the necessary training or experience to figure out every scenario we'll ever face. No one understands other people completely, much less their own self. We don't have the ability to be our own doctor when it comes to emotional, personal, or social issues.

I believe personal discontent with one's own life will keep a person from being there for other people. We do not have to be at our best to be present for others. Things will never be in perfect balance, so we cannot waste precious years attempting to get it together on our own. Before you know it, several years will have passed, and your loved ones won't know your status. Consider the following alternatives to remaining in isolation:

- Start the journey by learning about those around you.

- Make an effort to be a blessing to other people.

- Open up about traumatic experiences from the

past.

- Get accountability for communication, like a weekly call or text.

Gary Chapman identified five love languages that we use to express commitment—gifts, quality time, words of affirmation, acts of service, and physical touch.[4] Men need to be willing to take the time to learn how the people closest to them receive love. If we are disconnected, we aren't speaking or learning anyone's love language. And what's worse, we don't know our own. I want men to understand that you are robbing yourselves by being disconnected. It's better to be connected to people and make mistakes along the way and learn from them than to avoid people altogether out of fear you might make a mistake and let someone down.

It's a benefit to be connected to people. The blessings of openness, honesty, and vulnerability come back tenfold. When we're not lone wolves, others can help us understand ourselves better. And they can help us to understand others better, too. The more we understand ourselves and the more we appreciate others, the better friend, father, boyfriend, husband, and son we're able to be.

Deal with what's going on internally so you can be a blessing to other people. Take time to listen to other people. Take time to connect to other people, even if it's just to let them speak to you. Show yourself to be available.

CHAPTER FOUR

Myth #2—Distractions Are Solutions

As presidential candidates are now advocating for the legalization of marijuana, it is becoming broadly socially acceptable to smoke weed. As a native of the DMV (D.C., MD, and VA), I must say that we beat the presidential hopefuls to the punch. Smoking weed has been normal there for several years. In fact, I would be hard-pressed to find a peer from the area who does not or has not smoked.

However, if you take a step back and look at why young men are using marijuana, something darker emerges. The reality is that, more often than not, they are using marijuana as a coping mechanism. Based on my experience, one hundred percent of the men I know who smoke weed have unresolved trauma, and most of them either have an absent father, a toxic father, or a present-but-distant father.

There could be other things at play, but there is no denying the fact that if you have to depend on a substance to get through the day, something is not right. Our bodies weren't made to need the support of weed to get by. If there is a medical prescription for it, that's one thing, but

44 · MALIEK BLADE

when we play doctor for ourselves in this way, we never get healed. The wake and bake lifestyle has become the norm for far too many of us. However, I want to affirm that life without the support of weed is achievable. Wake and bake and a blunt to get to bed may be your reality now, but it does not have to be your future.

Distractions Compound the Issue

Distractions are attempts at solutions for many men because we don't know how to deal with the root of a problem. We simply use something else to take our attention off the issue at hand. These issues may be due to frustration caused by an absent father, sadness or brokenness over a relationship that ended, or perhaps the loss of a job. They may be caused by the passing of a loved one, such as a mother. Whether our issues are the unfortunate consequences of our own decisions or due to frustration from a circumstance that was out of our control, we must deal with, cope with, and resolve said issues head-on. In most other areas of life, we encourage men to be direct, yet we excuse a passive approach when it comes to dealing with our personal issues.

Weed

To eradicate the need for harmful distractions, it's important to first acknowledge that there is a problem. It's not healthy, and it is not sustainable. Why? Some issues work themselves out, so for some, getting high helps them not to worry while they are waiting. However, some things do not change until you man up and make a direct move by creating a resolution.

The goal should be to move away from depending on the substance and to deal with trauma, hurt, frustration, loss, or failure. The problem with using a substance to

forget the difficulties in your life is that reality is
waiting for you. When you get high, you're only hig
that moment. Eventually, you're going to come do
from the high, and whatever issue you were trying to forget about will still be there. If you keep getting high, you
won't make any progress in dealing with the issue, so
there will never be a solution.

Sex

The same thing can be said for sex. Many guys run to
sex for the instant gratification it provides. It's an easy
way to feel affirmed, valued, and wanted. The reality is
that a lot of men can have sex without an emotional connection. It's not about being connected to the person; it's
about what the person can do for your benefit. It provides
a distraction in a stressful situation. Of course, it's stress
relief in the physical sense, but it is also something positive that you can focus on while you are trying to avoid
something negative. Once again, every sexual experience,
just like drugs, creates a high you'll eventually come
down from. The sensation doesn't last forever. The eu-
phoric feelings that come from a sexual experience are
only temporary. Once again, sex is not an efficient problem solver, as it does nothing in terms of creating a
resolution.

Not only do we need to stop using sex as a distraction,
we need to safeguard it more. Sex shouldn't be freely
given to just anyone. I say this because I have seen casual
sex that is meant to be a distraction from one issue create
another set of issues. Have you ever agreed with a partner
that your relationship would be solely physical, yet somewhere along the way one party still ends up catching
feelings? A transactional approach to sex can also create
a new set of personal problems, like contracting an STD
or creating a child you weren't planning on. With a new

and no practical steps for a solution, you
hamster on the wheel, exerting plenty of
ıg no real progress. This is how we find
ng the same cycles in our lives—we
distractions instead of resolving the is-

Games

Another common escape for men is video games.
Gaming is on the rise, and you'll hear women complain
about guys who spend all their time on the game. The
game is an escape from reality, literally creating a false
world with goals and rewards that don't translate to real
life. Spending time in this false reality, getting away from
the real world and creating a separate world where you
can be successful and win, gives you a sense of gratification when you don't feel like you're winning in your
personal life.

I can hear the naysayers now: "It's not that deep," or
"There's nothing wrong with playing video games."
Gameplay is not inherently bad, but with a bit of research,
you'll find that it is a growing compulsive behavior that
affects other areas of life. With the exception of those who
play games professionally, there is a problem with individuals spending an extensive amount of time doing
something that has no effect on real life while ignoring
real life issues.

To the man who has balance and is actively dealing
with his issues while playing games in moderation for entertainment, I salute you, but so often that is not the case.
The game usually comes at the expense of something else.
I am not saying you should never play games. I am saying
games should be considered a luxury, something to do after you have taken care of your primary priorities.

Alcohol

The last example is drinking. Some people say that social drinking isn't a bad thing, and I agree with that. But let's be real, most people don't drink because they enjoy the taste or because they're thirsty. People drink to feel something or to stop feeling something else. Many drink to get drunk. We shouldn't use social drinking as an excuse to cover up the real issue, which may be alcoholism. Yes, running to alcohol to cope indicates an unhealthy relationship with alcohol. Even if it's not alcoholism, your drinking is the direct result of your inability to cope with an issue.

Personally, I don't see the wisdom in getting drunk. When has being less conscious ever solved anything or been helpful? It only makes things worse. When you are less cognizant, you do things you wouldn't normally do, and you probably aren't going to remember them when you return to full consciousness. Nothing good ever comes from this. I believe many of us drink just because it's normal and commonly accepted, yet we disregard the effects. How many low points in your life or the lives of your friends were tied to alcohol? How many high points were tied to alcohol?

I know this specifically will be an unpopular view, but I believe that alcohol is not only an unhealthy coping mechanism, but it points to immaturity. How much can you trust an adult who is constantly putting himself in harm's way? When someone is consistently getting drunk, that makes him less able to lead, provide, and safeguard his family and others. A drunk is never fit to lead.

An Endless Cycle

If distractions draw you, you are creating a cycle of co-dependence. If one perceives manhood to be strength, courage, and leadership, then becoming dependent on drugs, sex, games, or alcohol is probably the least manly thing you can do. It shows a lack of discipline and self-control. It shows an inability to think an issue through logically and spiritually and deal with the root of the problem. It shows a dependence on escapism and avoidance.

Men are justifiably hard on other men who hurt women or kids and men who fold in the face of responsibility. Men like this are typically called cowards or punks. These labels are consistent with someone who exhibits escapist tendencies by running away from whatever the issue is and refusing to deal with it head-on. In the same way that a man would not suddenly become preoccupied with another task when a burglar is invading his family's home, we should not turn a blind eye toward the issues damaging our mental health by drinking, smoking, or sexing them away.

Sex, gaming, and drinking have their place and are not inherently wrong, but their misuse makes them a hindrance. Remember this life lesson—become an expert on your weaknesses as well as your strengths, then plan accordingly.

It's the Root Problem, Not the Enjoyment

The issue isn't necessarily the habit; it's what causes the habit. Why are you running to these things? My children's children would be born wealthy if I got ten dollars every time I heard the excuse, "I don't have a problem; I just like it. It feels good. I can stop whenever I want." If you ever see me in person, ask me how many of the people who told me this stopped drinking or smoking cold turkey. The "what" is the habit, but the "why" is the reason the habit exists. Once that is exposed, one can truly begin to break a habit.

You may feel it's not that deep, but as men, we often

say we're using logical thinking when we're oversimplifying so we can come to a perceived resolution quickly. We need to do the work of figuring out why we turn to certain substances and behaviors. We need to get used to asking and answering the hard questions about ourselves. Who hurt me? How did they hurt me? How did I deal with it? Did I deal with it in a healthy way? Who have I hurt? Why do I do things that hurt me? Do my actions show that I love myself? Do my actions reflect how I say I feel about my loved ones? Am I happy with who I am? Does my image on social media match my actual life, heart, and mind? Why? Why not?

We must ask ourselves these questions because even when we do not, the answers can reveal themselves very clearly to others. By this, I mean that insecurity is loud. There are passive and indirect aspects of what we do that expose what is going on in our minds and hearts. I am sure that I will get a lot of flak from the brothers for this, but I believe it's necessary to expose these things.

For the ladies, the following is a little insight for you. Most, if not all, men would like to be thought of as desirable by the opposite sex, even by women they may never sleep with. Our ability to draw women is a big part of what strokes our ego. How I feel about myself is almost directly correlated to how women deal with me. With that in mind, men go above and beyond to be perceived a certain way or "look good," even if what is being portrayed is not true.

In the age of social media, social media accounts have become billboards to market yourself to potential mates. We often joke about how women use filters, makeup, fake hair, Photoshop, twerking, and thirst traps to look more desirable. We confidently label this insecurity, but men do the same thing in less obvious ways. Whether it is strategically placing a Magnum condom in the background or foreground of a picture on Instagram or pretending that a visible erection is a flaccid print, we do odd things to get attention and feel wanted as well. The relevance is that craving attention from strangers can be tied to a lack of attention or affirmation at home during one's developmental years. The same can be said for a man who is feeling unwanted in his marriage. A wife's denial of sex can easily lead to a husband posting to social media just for the likes and comments. We want to be wanted, and we will search high and low for that affirmation until we get it.

If trauma rocked your world as a child and you start therapy when you're thirty-five, you may not remember as much of the original trauma. You may not even understand exactly how you felt in that moment or what damage was done to you, and the parties that may have played a role in your traumatic experience may not even be around anymore. While it's never too late for therapy, you may be left unable to reconcile certain things if you wait too long.

Some steps must be taken with haste. A preacher I know didn't have much of a relationship or connection to his dad until his father was on his deathbed. He reconciled with him in the hospital. Not everyone is lucky enough to have a last-minute reunion. Reconnecting during someone's last moments of life is not ideal, either. Why wait? Why put it off? Not being able to deal with broken relationships and potentially not having the opportunity to reconnect with the person may be even more traumatic than the rift between you.

Aside from a man running from his own trauma, the biggest hindrance to men getting to their root issues is the lack of a father or father figure. Often, we as men make our own decisions while having a select few we look to for guidance. Our dad should be in that select few. From his position of power and influence, he could easily step in and draw his son's attention to the root issues and help him—in a perfect world, that is. However, with a lack of fathers and father figures, guys walk alone, miss out on the wisdom of others, repeat cycles, and never resolve deep personal issues.

A Solution That Works

You do not have to suppress things or "suck it up," as some have told you. While statements like that are an attempt at nobility and strength, they are actually idiotic because they leave no room for conflict resolution. Pretending that hurt or frustration isn't there does not make the hurt or frustration go away. You can address the problem, work through its effects on you, and come out stronger than before because you had a problem that you resolved rather than allowing the problem to destroy you. The following three steps will lead you to freedom:

Step #1. Acknowledge and accept that while turning to drugs, casual sex, obsessive gaming, and binge drinking is normal for many, it is not ideal or healthy. If you do not want your family to follow the path of a stereotypical black family, ready yourself to be the outlier, then lead the way. Avoidance is unfit for a leader. It's unfit for a father. It's unfit for a husband. Be the one to set the tone for dealing with personal issues in your circle and in your house.

Face the issue with assertive strength. If you deal with your problems head-on, morally and boldly, you set the tone of healthy behavior for your family. They'll see that you're not an escapist and not in bondage to addictive behaviors, which will give them a renewed idea of what is possible and what is acceptable. As fathers, we can only replicate what we are. Our children duplicate what they see. But it starts with you.

Step #2. Seek help to resolve the issues that are holding you back. Our strength does not give us all the answers. Our insight is limited in scope. To grow, we need help from others. That may include ongoing advice from a

trusted person; sessions with a licensed professional coun-
selor, therapist, or psychologist; spiritual advice from a
church leader or pastor; or insight from a formal mentor.
I get it! As an adult, it's difficult to build these types of
relationships and be fully transparent about who you are
and what you've been through. I believe it's more beneficial to take the harder approach than to suppress, isolate,
and hope for the best. Opening up to others can be helpful
in determining what caused the trauma and probing for the
root of what you're trying to get away from.

Also, talking to the people who may have offended you
can lead to understanding. Old issues are typically seen as
unimportant because we think if it's out of sight, then it's
out of mind. However, we all need someone to talk to and
be fully transparent with. This person may not be in your
immediate circle, but you must get what you need for you.
Perhaps your father wasn't affectionate enough. Your
problem may be a mother who put her career first, or
maybe it's a relationship that went bad.

Finding the roots of the pain and frustration by talking
out the problem is a powerful and necessary part of becoming the man you need to be.

Step #3. Address the issues head-on. Through step two,
you'll find out what has been affecting you and why. With
a better idea of what happened, you can move forward accordingly rather than having a blurred view of whatever
the issue is and running to drugs, sex, gaming, or drinking
to just block it out. Go back and have conversations to
give yourself closure so you're not living with a whole
bunch of what-ifs. With this newfound knowledge, you
must then do something different. This could be changing
a friend group, cutting someone off, or establishing new
relationships with different types of people. Simply knowing isn't enough. Once you know the ailment, you must
seek to heal.

CHAPTER FIVE

Myth #3—Street Loyalty

Some call it "the hood." Others say it's the "inner city." But for many born into that area, it's just home. And most of the guys who grow up there eventually accept that life beyond the hood isn't attainable. They consider their dreams, life goals, relationships, and plans to be limited to the boundaries of that under-resourced, crime-filled, densely populated area.

If a hood dude wants to get married, he plans to marry someone in the neighborhood or someone from the area. If he wants to pursue a career, he looks for jobs nearby. The issue is, the inner-city residents often lack resources and access intentionally. You don't see people of status moving nearby until gentrification begins, the neighborhood is remodeled, and you are pushed out.

Sports, we're told, will get us into college with the possibility of getting a full-ride scholarship and moving on to professional ball. If you make the cut, you're set for life. If sports aren't your thing, there's always a career in rap. Outside of that, things seem bleak.

Inner-city guys grow up believing these are the best possible outcomes for their future. They don't think more is possible. They set the bar low when planning their lives because the scope of the future is limited by what they see. They don't aspire to do more beyond their borders because all they know is that the top tier men in that area seem to be the drug dealers or people who are in gangs. They are the respected or feared men in the community, and youth often settle for that and think, *"Well, that's what I want to be."*

This is where the myth of street loyalty comes in. It's a two-fold belief system.

1. In order to "keep it real," I must stay connected to the things and people I grew up with.

2. If I do find success, I must bring those I grew up with me or I am being "Hollywood" or "brand new."

The desire for success is there. However, street loyalty comes with a level of limited optimism that restricts what could be to certain things involving certain people. This is fully beneficial for those in proximity to someone who finds success and the ability to move out of the hood, but it leaves the successful person with many strings attached. He's forced to stay in the hood or bring the hood with him. Somehow, not doing one or the other makes you a sellout. You have seen this play out in the news when a successful rapper is touring the country, but he's still involved in gang activity or he chooses to bring his associates from the drug game on as his entourage.

A Toxic Mindset

If Dad is not there or he does not speak up, the mindset of the boy is shaped to the culture of neighborhood and the things he can do to be accepted by his peers. Because the neighborhoods are typically not in good shape, the residents are not very hopeful concerning the future. The success stories are typically guys who got out due to putting work into their sport. Outside of that, drug dealers stand out because they're able to buy nice things. A young boy in his formative years sees that and wants it. He wants success, and that is what success looks like in his context. Our boys have a limited scope of what could be, so the bar is set low. They're robbed of the opportunity to imagine or hope for more. In the rare cases that they get more, they are pressured to carry the baggage of past people and habits with them.

This was seen in more recent times when Michael Vick, a successful NFL quarterback, was involved in illegal dog fighting.[5] He had to bring along something from his past that he felt comfortable with, and despite the money, the fame, and the prestige that he achieved legally, he still felt as if he needed to be involved with something illegal yet familiar. Street loyalty can also be seen as blind commitment to certain outlooks or habits, even to one's own detriment. You take it with you even though you've ascended beyond your previous circumstances, even beyond your wildest dreams. You can be a millionaire but still returning to the things that are normal, comfortable, or familiar. It is okay to let go. It is okay to completely disconnect from things or people of the past.

The Mindset of Possibility

It's time to do away with ideas that keep a brother bound even when he reaches a new level in life. You can keep it real and be wise by remembering that:

1. Loyalty to people does not require commitment to a location. You can be from the South Bronx with a passion to give back to the community and relocate your family at the same time. While there is a benefit to anchoring yourself there, you have the freedom to choose. When choosing, consider whether staying will have you being a positive impact on the community or the community and people being a negative influence on you. Each person is different.

2. There is much more to life. There are several possibilities outside of what you've seen in the town where you were born and raised. Never box yourself in or limit your potential based on others. This is not to say that it's easy to overcome the odds and do something bigger or better with your life, but it is possible.

3. Cutting certain people off is perfectly fine. As we mature and receive new opportunities, we're confronted with the complex reality of change. You may have done dirt with a certain group in the past, but eventually you may recognize the error of your ways. Realizing this and making changes is not being fake and does not give people permission to shame you into staying the same. Also, not all old friends should go with you into new places. The deciding factor is what they are bringing to the table. You may both have made mistakes together in the past, but if you're on a new page and they're still doing the same old stuff, they could corrupt your new situation. You can't allow that. Help where you can while protecting your situation.

On an individual basis, we can take the responsibility as men to cast a wider net and paint a broader and more diverse picture for these young men, showing what's possible for them beyond what they've seen.

CHAPTER SIX

Myth #4—Emotions
Are Feminine

Many men go through their whole lives without ever really stopping to process through their emotions. They stay at level five (cliché) and four (facts) communication both with themselves and with others. Not only do we often lack the skill sets or the tools to know how to process emotions, many of us are socialized to dislike emotions. Emotions are seen as the enemy of progress and the less productive path compared to logical thinking.

Men are often taught to suppress emotions to avoid appearing weak or feminine. We are taught to think that women are naturally overly emotional, but I think that women feel more confident and comfortable expressing how they feel because they are encouraged to do so by the other women in their lives. It's time to break the myth that emotions are a sign of weakness. It's time to embrace the truth that emotions are a sign of humanity rather than a sign of femininity. However, before we as men learn how to share our emotions with others, we need to be able to process them personally in a mature way.

The Extreme Degrees of Emotions in Men

One of the results of this myth is that men tend to end up in one of three camps when it comes to emotions. At one extreme are the men who don't share emotions at all. They are completely bound up and locked inside, making it impossible for them to connect with others. These are the lone wolves we spoke of earlier. At the other extreme are men who are overdoing it with emotions. These men are comfortable publicly sharing emotion, but they reserve expression for feelings of anger, which are demonstrated by acts of force or aggression. Somewhere in the middle are men who share emotions, but they think it's only appropriate to share their feelings with the women they are dating or with their wives, unfairly burdening them with all of their emotional baggage.

Whatever camp they fall into, these men aren't dealing with their emotions properly. The idea that having emotions or being emotional is a feminine trait robs men of the opportunity to be fully themselves and turns them into mere robots—receiving and giving information independent of unique thoughts, feelings, or concerns.

Emotions aren't exclusively for women. They are for humans. They're something that we all have but process in different ways. Men hurt in silence after years of suppressing emotions. Even after acknowledging this problem, it continues because many of us believe that this is what it means to be a man. When we remember that distractions are not solutions, we are then more open to a newfound perspective on manhood that acknowledges and manages personal emotions and the emotions of our loved ones. True masculinity is being able to express emotion in a healthy way. Emotions aren't just for women, but our emotional maturity is needed all the more when connecting with a woman.

Emotions in Relationships

Emotions do not only affect the person feeling them; they affect everyone around that person. For example, it's almost impossible for a woman to connect deeply with a man who is not in touch with his emotions or who doesn't understand his emotions. Many women settle for an acquaintance type relationship where the two share time, space, and their bodies but never fully know each other. There are countless stories of sisters feeling like the man they're living with has built up a wall between them. We take pride in performing physical intimacy but often fall short when it comes to emotional intimacy. Emotional intimacy goes much deeper than physical intimacy. You can know how someone looks and even how they taste and smell but still not know who they are.

It's easy to recognize the problems with hiding your emotions in dating and marriage, but not so clear is the damage done when a father hides his emotions from his children. The man who is emotionally tough or believes that emotions are for women ends up being the present-but-distant father. It not only affects his sons, but it also affects his daughters. When daughters experience this, they are likely to seek out affection from other men because they didn't get it from their father, which is one of the reasons the term "daddy issues" is often associated with women who are seen as needy or promiscuous.

So, the cat is out the bag—men have feelings about everything that is said about them or done to them. We feel good when someone speaks highly of us or affirms our skills or when new people come into our lives who are supportive. We feel hurt when we lose people or don't get a job or when terrible injustices seem to rule the day. There are feelings attached to every aspect of our lives, and we need to understand this in order to be able to communicate what we're feeling and why.

Managing Emotions

Emotional awareness is an asset for men because someone who is unable to manage or understand his emotions is susceptible to having his emotions manipulated by someone else. Someone who is able to think through his emotions in a logical way can be measured in his response. He isn't going to get played easily or tricked into certain damaging reactions because he is in control by being proactive rather than reactive. If you are under the spell of believing that emotions are for women and you aren't aware of your emotional experiences, you give strangers the opportunity to control you.

An example of this is often seen with men who are unable to think strategically because emotions control their decisions. They mistakenly believe that they are in control because they've buried their feelings when in reality their emotions are at play, causing them to respond a certain way to the situations in which they find themselves.

If you put the antics and some of the silly characters he's played aside, actor Terry Crews is thought of as an intimidating-looking dude. He recently came forward to admit that he was sexually assaulted by an agent.[6] The agent was at a party and grabbed his groin with Terry's wife present. Terry says he jumped out of shock, and he told some of the other people at the party about the experience. More recently, Terry has had to navigate through pushback from various sides, publicly.

When Terry came forward, he was criticized by a lot of other black men who said he should have beaten that guy up. They questioned why Terry let him get away with groping him, and Terry is now seen by some as less than masculine because he was the victim and because he came forward with charges that he was assaulted.

What many wanted Terry to do was to act out of emotion, to get frustrated and angry and beat the man down.

Terry's ultimate response in coming forward was more strategic. He recognized that he would be perceived as an intimidating, musclebound, dangerous black man. He is working in a mostly white industry. If, in that moment, he had beaten up an agent who sexually assaulted him, he understood that the narrative could easily have flipped to a story about an angry black man beating up a white agent. It could also have been perceived as a hate crime because he beat up a gay man.

These are all potential consequences that could have happened if Terry had just responded with a knee-jerk re-action, being unwise with how he stewarded his emotions. But he thought about strategy. He thought about how he could potentially go to jail if he beat someone up, which would have affected him and his family. He was able to think more long term and work through the abuse and his emotions in a healthy way. Terry stewarded his emotions in accordance with his strategy and long-term goals rather than letting an impulsive—albeit justifiable—reaction take over. It's not just about emotion; it's about strategy and the impact of our decisions.

It's important to remember that aggression ends up having a long-term impact. Instead of thinking about the future, we just think in the moment and of the satisfaction in avenging ourselves. This is unhealthy emotional man-agement at work.

If you aren't managing your emotions well, you can make a bad decision that not only affects you but affects your wife or girlfriend or daughter or son or whoever else is important in your life. In Terry's case, he is the bread-winner for his family. One off night, one frustrating moment, one mistake, could have resulted in him throw-ing everything away. With this kind of pressure on men, we must be fully aware of just how connected we are to our emotions. We cannot allow our need to appear tough outweigh our family's need for us.

Our emotions are there. They are active. They affect why we do the things we do.

Embracing Emotion

Although America may be at a point culturally where pro-gay is the way, that perspective is typically not shared by the average American living in the inner city. Realistically, black men from the inner city still hold traditional yet questionable views of masculinity and sexuality, which can be toxic in some ways. For most of us, weakness and femininity in men are considered synonymous with homosexuality. This false thinking is part of why we run so far from emotion, but I'll unpack that more in a later chapter. That same fear is projected on to our sons. I've seen fathers embrace ineffective courses of action to ensure their sons are strong and straight.

I remember a family friend who wanted to make sure that his son was tough. He took his eight-year-old and punched him in the chest. Again. And again. And again. Standing over him, he commanded the boy not to cry. PUNCH. "Don't cry." PUNCH. "You don't cry, boy." And that was his way of ensuring that his son was tough and not weak.

How does punching him repeatedly guarantee he won't be weak or feminine? It just makes the son fear his father while further damaging the son. Abusive behavior sets a son up to be weak rather than strong because it causes emotional trauma that will affect how he approaches every situation later on in life. Right now, he doesn't understand. You are confusing him because his dad, who is supposed to love him, is also abusing him. This isn't disciplining rebellious behavior. This is abuse. All because his dad's own fear, which is emotional, hasn't been thought through clearly or dealt with in a healthy manner.

Emotions are normal. They're wonderful. Falling in

love. Feeling respected. The bond in brotherhood. A tournament win. Getting a raise. A mother's love. You and your father sharing moments in the latter part of his life. These situations offer the opportunity to experience life at its best. You want people to feel good about you. You want your significant other to affirm you. You want your children to respect you and speak highly of you when they are in public. These are all emotional things. They are not just transactions. You don't want your children to just do what you say and see you as an authority figure with whom they have no personal connection. Being an authoritarian is not the same thing as being a father.

We have to step back and reflect on our emotions in a logical way to ensure we aren't doing toxic and damaging things to our sons just because we feel a certain way in the moment. Emotional maturity is an area that we've been allowed to fail in for years.

Your humanity is a gift. Don't be afraid of your emotions. Enjoy them. However, enjoy them responsibly, not at the expense of the future.

CHAPTER SEVEN

Myth #5—Boys Will Be Boys

I was just listening to an interview on the Breakfast Club. It's a nationally syndicated hip hop radio show based out of New York City, and the guest was movie producer Devon Franklin.[7] He was promoting a book on the truth about men, and he was talking about men needing to do the work of getting their minds and emotions straight before they try to connect with a woman. One of the co-hosts of the show, Charlamagne Tha God, began thinking out loud.

He shared that he is working to become a better person, and he said that, over the past few years, he has been faithful to his wife and has been going to therapy. He has been drinking less, staying away from drugs, and eating healthy and working out. Having done all these things to better himself, he admitted, "I think around thirty-five I started to do the work. Thirty-seven is when I finally said, 'You have to be the change you want to see in the world.'"[8]

I applaud the brother for starting somewhere, but thirty-five is very late. At the age of thirty-five, he already had children and a wife. That means he spent several years damaging the woman he is married to as well as others in his life. He has since admitted to this. Look beyond yourself for a minute. Your wife, kids, and loved ones need you to start this process of becoming the man you should be as early as possible. Otherwise, they end up becoming the victims of your immaturity. There is nothing enlightened about waiting to put away childish things. Consider the example Charlamagne set for the people who were watching him. He will admit that he didn't have the best example from his dad. His dad cheated on his mom, and he despised him for that, but he ended up imitating his dad. He ended up being the thing he hated most. He continued the cycle.

This story is far from rare. We aren't waking up and realizing the urgent need to leave childish ways in childhood rather than holding on to them throughout adulthood. It's time for us to realize that we must be considerate of the people we're connected to, especially the women. We do a disservice to the men around us by affirming bad behavior and allowing it to continue in their youth instead of correcting it. It's time to stop attributing the problematic behavior to the tired old trope of "boys will be boys." We must not turn a blind eye to bad behavior because a guy is young or encourage it in adulthood. We know that black boys are often seen as men before the age of eighteen.

Damage Done

We expect young women to be mature relatively early and to be chaste until later in life, but we don't hold our boys to the same standards. The assumption is that young men are going to do what young men do.

It's up to us to set the bar higher for being a young man. Unfortunately, young manhood is currently associated with reckless decisions and limitless freedom. This creates a culture that not only permits but encourages unhealthy behavior. Somehow, we've believed that we

WHOLE BROTHER · 67

can approve problematic actions in boys' younger years, and they will eventually grow out of it. Much of the grief our sisters face is because many of us never do grow out of it. We boldly carry problematic norms into a relationship. This is called prolonged adolescence, where you have older men still making the mistakes from their childhood because they haven't been shown the error of their ways. Others have been taught but have not yielded to the guidance of someone wiser.

Often, the myth of "boys will be boys" blocks out recognition of the need for maturity, and this is most visible in romantic relationships. Generally, we expect guys to have multiple sexual partners, and it's not really a big deal for a guy to get a young girl pregnant before he even has the means to provide for himself. The reckless behavior is considered okay because sex is just part of manhood. Right? Some of you know men with more baby mamas than Future but without even a fraction of Future's money. Someone's sex life and habits are their business until they affect us, like when Mom has to play daycare provider for her grandkids or when Dad's little girl becomes a single mom.

Most men will continue to make bad decisions if they aren't shown a better way. As the saying goes, "When you know better, you do better."

Rather than getting themselves together before they try to connect with a woman, young men expect women to put up with all their drama and baggage and unhealthy habits. For many, "ride or die" really means that she puts up with their BS and lack of preparation. Yes, I understand that relationships are a process people need to work through together and that no one is perfect. But just because we are fallible doesn't mean we lower the bar for just anybody.

Guys who have been taught that it's okay to be foolish in your youth continue those life practices with the women to whom they are connected. They're experimenting and seeing what they can get away with. With immaturity comes self-centered thinking. This mindset judges the quality of relationships based on how much they can get out of it without changing who they are and what they already do. Women who push back or demand better are considered high maintenance. This kind of guys wants a woman who says, "Boys will be boys," when he screws up. Tolerance is prioritized over growth and change. Men do not ask women to wait for them to grow up; boys do. In other words, when considering her, it is more noble to let her go while you work on yourself than to hold her hostage while you continue to damage and burden her.

Put in the Work

It's important for everyone in the culture to be *woke*. Being woke means having an awareness of black history, social inequality, and other issues that face black people. When we're woke, we're cognizant of how challenges play out systematically and culturally, how we're connected to the community, and how being a part of the remedy for issues improves the lives of everyone around us. But it's hard for us to be woke if we're part of the problems that are damaging our community—specifically, hurting black women.

How woke can you be if you leave a trail of emotionally battered black women behind you? Not all relationships work, and we should seek to normalize drama-free mutual breakups that don't involve bickering and passive aggression. Women have their faults, and as a guy reading, you might be thinking about who she is and what she did. However, right now, I'm addressing the men. I'm addressing you. What did you do? Does she refer to you as a positive, motivating force like Aaliyah sang about, or are you a negative, discouraging force? We appreciate the words of our exes when they give us props on bedroom performance, but what will they say about our communication skills?

How is being woke relevant here?

Wokeness is about doing the personal work to be in a place where you can facilitate change. It's doing the research and making the connections with people. It's being more and doing more for the greater good. Compare the idea of being woke with the idea of being whole. You do the work of developing yourself as an individual. You're aware of your issues, your emotions, your relationships, and your career, and you make sure that your actions are not damaging your sisters and brothers. We don't normally think of wokeness in these terms because our focus is on accomplishing social justice goals, preaching the message of freedom, advancing certain polices, getting people involved politically, raising money, and giving back. All these things are beautiful and needed, but we often do all this public woke work without doing any personal woke work. Unbeknownst to us, we as men attempt to compensate for our personal bad with public good. We use our social justice efforts to try to cancel out our private evil instead of doing the personal work to become better men.

Three Areas of Development

Physical development is not the only sign of manhood. Mental, emotional, and professional development also indicate that a boy is becoming a man. Often, we just focus on muscles and strength. And why not? When we're full of life and power, once we've grown tall, once hair has started growing on our bodies, once we've built muscle and our voices have deepened, we want to test our strength. We equate physical development with manhood.

Sometimes, however, we forget about mental

development. It's really unfortunate to see men who are fully physically developed but have chosen to remain preteens mentally. We forsake the inside and devote ourselves to developing the outside. Our lack of development in the following areas tends to be why others reach out for support in those same areas. My actions as a result of not going to therapy could very well end up pushing you to go to therapy. Growth and development in the following areas will not make life perfect, but they are enough to provide a firm foundation on which to build. The transition from boyhood to manhood is marked by growth in these three areas:

Head (Mental Health). A mentally unstable person is a liability to others. As men, we must take responsibility for getting our minds right. We need to be clear on where we're going, what we're doing, and why. Health in this area is most clearly demonstrated when you are influencing for positive purposes rather than being influenced for negative purposes. Additionally, even though being in a constant battle with your own thoughts is normal for many, it's not a safe place to be. It is our responsibility to take our internal battles seriously and seek the proper professional help.

Heart (Emotional Maturity). The emotional spectrum covers much more than anger. We must be able to understand and communicate what we are feeling in a mature way. Punching walls is inappropriate, as is screaming, assuming the worst, and projecting what others did onto a new person. These are all emotionally immature habits that typically go unchecked, and we are not usually aware that we're doing them. Health in this area is demonstrated by the ability to continue a relationship after an offense. Cutting people off or falling back when something goes wrong robs you of the opportunity to grow emotionally.

Hands (Professional Advancement). Whether through entrepreneurship or working a normal nine to five job, every man must be able to provide for himself first and then others later. Through legal means, a man needs to obtain consistent income and a home of his own. This is base level independence. Professional advancement starts here and goes far beyond to employing others. Anywhere within the spectrum is a fine spot to land, as we all are different. Health in this area is demonstrated by being able to cover the basic needs and have money to spare.

Rather than giving our boys a pass for bad behavior when they're young, let's start them on the fast track to manhood in their teens. It is never too soon to start being more responsible and more considerate.

CHAPTER EIGHT

Myth #6—Therapy Is for Crazy People

The way I was raised, therapy wasn't an option unless you wanted to be labeled crazy. There was a racial dynamic to this—a perception that therapy was something white people did. I remember hearing the statement, "Black people don't have the time to be depressed." That said, the feeling that therapy is for crazy people goes beyond the borders of the inner city. I have heard of friends' family members who don't want to go despite displaying traits of bipolar disorders, depression, and more.

Many problems could be easily fixed if a mental health professional was allowed to offer a solution. Instead, people are told to go to church more or pray more. While I do think spiritual elements help to a certain extent, I don't think the church is an appropriate replacement for therapy. God provides doctors, therapists, and medication for us to use for a reason. Keep in mind that although church and therapy do not replace each other, they can work well alongside each other.

The Power of Social Stigma

My former role as a dean of students at a university allowed me to speak to quite a few students about disciplinary issues. When corrective measures are needed, it's normally tied to a broken rule. And when someone breaks a school rule, it's typically because there's a personal issue at the root of it. In my experience, white students were always more open to counseling or therapy than black male students were.

I remember walking through the disciplinary process with a black male who believed he was depressed. He definitely showed symptoms, and he believed his depression played a part in why he had an infraction and falling grades. I suggested, "Well, you feel that you are depressed, but you haven't been given a proper diagnosis. So, you should probably see a professional to have that diagnosis and see what you can do from there." Although the possibility of depression was putting his grades in jeopardy and affecting his life dramatically—even getting him sent to my office for an infraction—he still said to me, "I don't know. I don't want anyone to call me crazy."

So even though he felt like his life was falling apart and he was damaged and hurting, he still did not want to be labeled and was not open to seeking out professional help. The stigma of labels like "crazy" and other misrepresentations is so strong that we avoid the help we so desperately need. I have heard another fear, that once you get labeled, you're labeled forever. There is a fear that if you do go to a therapist or if you do go to get professional help, that will somehow put a note on your permanent record that sticks with you forever. You won't get a job. People will avoid you. They'll think something is wrong with you.

There are a lot of misunderstandings related to therapy and counseling, and the myth needs to be dispelled. First, going to therapy doesn't mean you're crazy. In fact, going to therapy can be the thing that keeps you from going crazy. It means that you're taking charge of your life and seeking to improve it. You may have weak areas in your life but seeking help doesn't mean you're broken beyond repair. There is strength in having enough self-awareness to realize that you do not have the strength to face and overcome certain things on your own. Saying "I'm good" and failing as you go forward is not success. Don't let your pride keep you stuck in the same spot for years. Therapy gives you the tools you need to work through your feelings, the problems you're facing, and if needed, the medication you need to manage your life.

Breaking the Stigma

I'm not the only one who notices this. The same radio personality I mentioned earlier, Charlamagne Tha God, agrees. His most recent book, titled *Shook One: Anxiety Playing Tricks on Me*, is a transparent account of his experience with mental health issues and his journey to awareness.[9] One of his stated intents is to break the stigma surrounding mental health issues in the black community. The whole book is dedicated to the one myth I'm addressing here. He talks about his anxiety attacks. He talks about parental paranoia, worrying about the worst possible things happening to his children. We have widely accepted the idea that therapy isn't for us. He discussed his preference for seeing a therapist who is from a completely different racial background so that the therapist can listen with an unbiased view. I believe having an outsider's view is a good thing to a point. I also think that, to a certain extent, it's beneficial to have someone fully understand where you are coming from. Sometimes cultural differences can impair the judgment of the therapist. Either way, it's something worth thinking about as you proceed.

The first person you see may not be a fit, but there are plenty of mental health professionals to choose from.

What's Really Going On?

Often, the fear related to therapy is not simply about being labeled. It's also about dealing with the issues.

Some of us intentionally stay busy so that we never have to deal with our personal issues. We stay preoccupied with building a business, trying to sell a product, trying to make a certain amount of profit, or trying to grow our savings. We throw ourselves into dating, traveling, hobbies—any excuse to avoid dealing with the issues that are bothering us so that we never have to feel the weight of the issue or revisit the pain.

I will say that in this stage of my life, the past couple of years have been the freest and most liberating because I took the time to sit down with a therapist to talk through some things. One takeaway that stood out to me came from a session when I spoke to my therapist about feeling like I cared too much.

As I spoke, I talked about being labeled as mature for my age and how that affected my relationships with others. I think the difficulties I faced were due to my functioning with a framework that wasn't normal amongst men of my race and age. Also, I spend a lot of time thinking through relationships, specifically my friendships, in this new way that I am presenting in this book.

Most guys are not familiar or comfortable with caring so much. These differences put a strain on many of my friendships, so I wish I didn't care so much about people or about maintaining relationships. Whether it's male friendships or female friendships, I want to be supportive.

When I see a flaw or a shortcoming, I want to help the person overcome it. I've never been the friend who minds their own business. I want to help them deal with their personal issues on a deep level because that was done for me and it made such a significant difference in my life. I don't care for small talk. I care to encourage my friends to do the work to resolve the thoughts and concerns they've chosen to suppress. Most guys would not describe themselves this way. I noticed and felt like an outlier. I thought something was wrong with me. Those sessions were the difference between me going left and adopting a "f*** it" mentality with people and going right and writing this book. Here we are!

I went into the therapy session asking the therapist if— more like telling the therapist—I just needed to care less. I wished I didn't care so much. The therapist turned my fears on their head by saying, "I don't think you're exhibiting traits that denote that care has become overbearing or too much. Your goal shouldn't be to care less. Your focus should be on properly stewarding the gift of care that you have."

What did that even mean? We went on to talk about a variety of scenarios that I have gone through with family, close friends, and acquaintances, and the conclusion lies in understanding the nuances of each situation. I care for people. Why take that away? I've taken a stance that is likely clear at this point. We as black men shouldn't be seeking to care less. We all could and should care more. It starts with selflessly taking interest in someone else. Our preconceived notions about people sometimes act as roadblocks to getting to know them. But once we understand where they are coming from, our relationship with them can grow deeper.

I had several sessions, but that one in particular resonated with me in such a way that I left the office feeling the freedom of truly understanding something that had perplexed me for years.

Because I broke through my fears about therapy, ignoring the myth, I was able to make connections regarding my issues that changed my life. I had someone from outside of my life looking at all the information I presented. It was important to have someone who was trained and experienced give their professional opinion.

The moment was so beneficial and pivotal for me that it planted the seed for this book. Therapy may provide the answers or give you the strength to do something special as well.

Be Free

As I said before, therapy isn't for crazy people. Rather, it can be the key to keep you from going crazy. Therapy can also be the catalyst that helps you live a free life. Many people, specifically black men, walk around with a chip on their shoulder. I understand that there are things that frustrate you and certain injustices you can't change or undo. However, therapy can directly affect your mood and your perspective. Even if you are in less than desirable circumstances and those circumstances do not change, a new perspective on them could be just the thing that helps you to cope and move forward.

What else can therapy do for you?

Therapy Can Show You a New Perspective

Our perspective is often more important than the subject being perceived. Perception affects how we handle our problems. If we never take the time to talk to someone else about our issues, we limit our breadth of perception.

I often left my therapy sessions with a new perspective. By ignoring therapy, we miss out on tapping into a resource that can help us live happier and fuller lives. There are things in our heads about which we have drawn conclusions. Sometimes we oversimplify things and draw negative conclusions, and we hold on to that negative perspective for years. Getting another perspective on said issue could change your perspective and show you that you may lack nuance in how you think through things. Imagine that! We all can err by thinking things through the wrong way. We must open ourselves up to the opportunity to recognize this.

Therapy Can Help You Mend Fences

Some things have happened to you that are unresolved. Some things have happened to you that you barely remember. Not only can therapy be beneficial in exposing some of these issues that are affecting you, you may then be put in a position where you are able to have a conversation with other parties involved. This could result in a healing moment that may be freeing and helpful for them as well. Moreover, therapy can give you the tools to help you fix things.

I'm not going to say that digging through the past is always the best thing to do. Sometimes it forces you to relive traumatic experiences. That takes preparation. Or even if you are healing by talking about traumatic experiences with a therapist, others you reach out to when trying to mend fences might not be ready or able to discuss the trauma. Not everyone is on board in dealing with their issues. However, you need to do the due diligence for yourself as an individual in order to be whole and live an optimistic life. Repeated grief makes us pessimists. No one likes being around a hopeless person. You need closure, even if they don't. There is no reason to go through life frustrated about something that you could cure through therapy. Just by being exposed to new information, many people have been able to put the past behind them.

CHAPTER NINE

Myth #7—Fear Equals Respect

When I was younger, I had a friend who was following a certain rapper who always had a mean mug. The rapper's career was rising at the time, and his gimmick was hustling and how dangerous he was. He never smiled. He always looked angry on all his album covers and in his music videos.

One day, my friend announced to me and others, "I don't smile." And from then on, he didn't. All of a sudden, we never saw him grin. His smile was gone. Why?

Because he was trying to fit the bill of what was popular at the time. That particular rapper got the attention and respect of men for his rapping ability, and women wanted him too. And my friend wanted to emulate the rapper's intimidating style.

This is a defense mechanism from living in the hood. The mindset behind it is that the more intimidating you look, the less likely someone is to try you. The same thing happens in prisons. Habits picked up while living in hostile environments then become norms for life.

While it is an attempt at self-preservation, it's miserable because it produces a cycle. Everyone is trying to appear unbothered, hard, masculine, aggressive, and dangerous, even if that's not who they are on the inside. It's a façade.

Hip hop culture teaches us to honor the most dangerous guy. With fear, we've adopted a cheap, artificial version of respect. The goal is to be the intimidator rather than to be genuinely respected for good qualities. This plays out in the family dynamic as well. Sons who fear their fathers typically don't have a good relationship with them in adulthood, yet sons who respect their fathers stay connected to them for a lifetime.

The Pitfalls of Intimidation

Leading with intimidation does not transfer well into other areas of life.

Marriage

Intimidation has no place in marriage. You want your wife to love you, not be afraid of you. Even when it comes to authority or leading, you want her to respect you for your skill set and character, not be afraid that you might cause physical harm to her or others. Getting people to follow your lead because you're a threat is manipulation, not leadership. We must do the work of becoming men worth trusting instead of scaring others into submission.

Parenting

So many men have accepted intimidation as the proper approach to raising children. However, intimidation is not true leadership; it's just coercion. It's backing people into a corner and getting them to follow you out of fear of what you might to do if they don't go along with your wishes. This lacks courageous character, and it's not ideal for a person who is parenting. The children will pick up these traits and bring them into the next relationship they're in. They may in turn use these same intimidation tactics on you. Abusers use fear to maintain control. At the root of this behavior is personal insecurity.

We need to be very careful not to normalize the idea that manhood is synonymous with violence, intimidation, or being dangerous. While these things garner respect in some settings, they make it hard for children to develop a sense of trust. Hypothetically, if accusations of abuse do come, it's much easier for people to assume that you did whatever you are being accused of because of the reputation you've established.

Cultural Transition

The intimidation approach doesn't transfer to other social settings. Outside the inner city, intimidation will get you nothing but closed doors because you're seen as a hothead who lacks discipline. What may be considered manly and self-sufficient in the hood can be considered pushy, arrogant, annoying, and self-absorbed in other areas. Taking this approach to the workplace will land you in the office of human resources or fired. A more universally respectable approach is exhibiting kindness and compassion.

Social Media

On another level, we live in the social media age where your persona isn't just in a physical neighborhood. Now guys are also being intentional about presenting themselves in this toxically masculine way on social media. And while the image they present is meant to make themselves look tough and intimidating, they're setting themselves up for failure when it comes to other areas of their lives. Ultimately, the only people they're impressing are other men who are behaving in the same brutish manner. It's not impressive to people who are functioning on a different wavelength.

Once again, think long term and bigger picture. You're branding yourself and your image every time you post something online. Don't just think about branding yourself in the way that makes you appeal to the hood. One day, the hood won't be the hood anymore. Hood clout cannot be withdrawn from an ATM. Think about branding yourself in a way that will allow you to rise above the conditions of your home environment. Being courageous and wanting to stand out in a crowd for the right reasons will get you noticed, and you'll find the respect you crave in turn.

Respect Is Worth It

As a child, I left a private middle school to go to another private high school, and a big part of getting into these schools were recommendations from respected people who vouched for my character.

This world values word of mouth. "I know a guy...." "Hey, check out such and such, he is good with...." Word of mouth saves businesses money. Word of mouth creates strong relationships. Respect has a much greater return on investment than intimidation and fear. Respectability is credibility that has been earned.

Respect Takes Hard Work

Respect needs to be the priority, and respect is earned by treating others with respect and bringing something respectable to the table. Respect takes hard work, but it's worth it.

Earning respect requires taking an interest in people, investing in them, and doing the right thing even when others aren't looking. This helps you to establish good character. Having people's respect will get you into places that fear could never get you into.

Being a Whole Brother is synonymous with being a respectable man. It is my hope that the content of this book can be a roadmap for those men seeking to move from being intimidating to being respected.

CHAPTER TEN

Myth #8—Manhood Is a Natural Instinct

Being physically male and behaving like a man are two different things. We often assume that if one has male body parts, the details of how to act like a man automatically follow like some sort of natural instinct. Unfortunately, manhood ends up being caught rather than taught in the right setting. Many times, this sense of manhood is caught from celebrities rather than from personal relationships.

During my transition from middle school to high school, Lil Wayne began his rise to the top of the rap game as a solo artist. Even before his album *Tha Carter III* sold a million copies in a week, he claimed to be the best rapper alive. Everyone was aspiring to be and look like him, and if you look around the rap game today, you will see the implications of his influence. Some may give credit elsewhere, but I truly believe many black men with face tattoos, dreads, and torsos covered in tattoos adorned their bodies in this way because Lil Wayne made it cool. In addition to Chris Brown, Wiz Khalifa, Gucci Mane, Bow Wow, and Soulja Boy with the torso tattoos, many guys in my hometown of D.C. changed their look to fit more with Lil Wayne's because he was the guy women wanted and men wanted to be.

If you look at today's top rappers, you would be hard pressed to find one who does not have a torso covered in tattoos. I think we must give credit where it is due. I'm going to go out on a limb and say the images guys are getting tatted may not be ones they are truly passionate about. However, the aesthetic is perceived as something that makes you desirable, so we ink random things on our bodies just to get the look. Additionally, many of us didn't know about filet mignon until Lil Wayne presented it in a very different context. Not only did he influence how guys look, he also influenced how we think.

While this song may have been putting into words something that was already true, I do believe it set the tone for a new generation of men figuring out how to show up in the world. I am speaking of the song "Pussy, Money, Weed" by Lil Wayne.[10] It really is the motivation for many men. A good day is having one of the three, and a great day is having all three at the same time. The three things mentioned in the title aren't seen as an occasional pleasure but as assets that make a man a man. However, I beg to differ.

Lil Wayne's reality became the norm that impressionable young boys pursued. In other words, Lil Wayne raised a generation of black and brown boys. He will tell you himself that his life consisted of drugs, crime, death, and sexual promiscuity. He didn't sign up to be a role model; he is just a storyteller. He is not the problem; our broken homes are.

There is a popular clip on the internet in which Lil Wayne shared an account of an early sexual experience.[11] He said that at the age of 11, adults encouraged an older woman to perform oral sex on him, and she did just that. There was little to no outrage at this story. In fact, the responses I remember included, "Wow, he started young!" and guys wishing they had had a similar opportunity. Imagine if this story were about a grown man putting his face between the legs of an eleven-year-old girl while adults encouraged it.

Lil Wayne's story is an account of sexual abuse of a minor, although he says he loved it. Because of our flawed view of manhood, this experience is seen as a notch on his belt rather than a traumatic experience for his heart and mind. Who knows the full effect of Lil Wayne's life experiences on his mental and emotional health? Regardless, he is the man who made the soundtrack to life for the pivotal developmental years of many men today.

In some cases, hip hop culture is the biggest influence after the home, and, in other cases, it is more influential than the home. The only reason I did not follow suit is because I had an older brother to present a counter narrative on what manhood looks like. Our boys need options. Healthy options. They need guidance, and they need to be taught how to be men instead of catching performative masculinity.

Manhood Must Be Taught

Too often, society assumes that men naturally know what to do. When a man asks for help, he is thought to be weak or less of a man. But today's entertainment portrays manhood as hustling to accomplish the next task and making it look easy along the way.

We look at the gossip page headlines and see it's all about which celebrities are sleeping with each other. The celebrities become the role models, and it is so appealing to mimic what they are doing. As a result, we see a trend among our young people to race to get into a relationship and have sex and then move onto the next relationship.

However, just because we have the parts doesn't mean

we're ready for sex or even a relationship. We can't assume that males are ready for sex like hip hop portrays. Maybe Lil Wayne makes it look desirable, but you are not likely to find a doctor, therapist, or social worker who will endorse this behavior.

We need to teach our young males that having a one-night stand is different from being in a relationship. A relationship does not define a man, and neither does sex. There is no shortage of rappers, movie stars, or entertainers who change mates every few weeks. And the gossip pages jump on it again. The average guy does not realize that much of this is staged for increased notoriety. It's a career move.

A relationship causes us to consider the needs of others over our own. It is about getting to know someone and sharing our lives with each other. It's not about always being tough or following the trends of what hip hop tells us to do. It's about balancing sensitivity, masculinity, and self-control.

When we can learn to care for another person in a relationship and push aside our selfish desires, then we are ready to become fathers. Many artists use their child's mother as a status symbol—for example, to highlight their ability to sleep with an attractive woman. Having sex with her becomes the accomplishment and takes precedence over sustaining the relationship. When image is the focus, the child is not considered. With fatherhood comes the responsibility and commitment to be there for a child, and as we already discussed, being there extends beyond a mere physical presence. Being a dad means teaching our sons and daughters about real manhood.

It's okay to say we need help. It's okay to seek out strong, healthy men in our lives who can be role models. We assume that men have no weaknesses and that they are always hopeful, secure, and confident, leaving no room for doubt, frustration, or fear. But let's be real—that's only true in the manufactured images we see in TV and film.

If you are just taking your cues from prominent people within hip hop, then you're being trained indirectly by someone with whom you really have no connection.

Until manhood is taught, we will handle the aforementioned like immature boys. Stop assuming and teach manhood.

Sensitivity Can Work

Manhood is taught both indirectly and directly, both through direct lessons and through examples and perceptions. What constitutes normal manhood is based on what is presented to us—what's acceptable, and what women respond to. How men perceive successful modes of conduct and presentability redefines itself based on what women's response to masculinity is and what women deem appropriate. I do think women play a part in this because many times, men simply proceed with what will garner the most attention from women.

If being sensitive ever becomes popular, guys will adjust accordingly. Look at Drake, who is one of the top-selling rap artists right now. He is a bit different. His raps aren't brutish or aggressive; he leads with honest emotion. I think he is at the top of his game right now because he is bringing something different and new to the picture that is not consistent with musical content from other men in his profession.

The male fans are identifying with Drake as a man expressing a variety of emotions in his songs. He expresses how women have hurt him, and he articulates concerns and worries while also being somewhat confident and bold as a man who is at the top of his field as one of the highest-selling artists of today. I think Drake has risen the way he has because he tapped into something that many others haven't. He created a space for the sensitive, cool guy who understands his emotional journey and seeks attention from women without demanding it. Many guys who didn't fit the bill for being the tough guy, thug type have found a place to stand with Drake.

Take Control

There's no doubt that celebrities exert a lot of influence on our culture. But how does a man step away from mirroring a famous rapper and become his own man?

Manhood must be taught by fathers to sons. Someone who is not being taught by a father needs to be able to identify who is teaching them and whether what is being passed down is harmful or helpful.

Some things that are taught by rappers and other celebrities, such as verbal abuse and the objectification of women, must be unlearned. However, for someone to unlearn these things, they must be replaced by solid teaching.

Intentional learning is the best way to proceed. Be intentional about who you take pointers from. Be intentional about choosing to follow someone's lead. Be conscious of who you are following. If that's the first thing you do, you have already developed a wise habit in your life.

Ask yourself the following questions:

- Where did I pick this up from?
- Who did I pick this up from?
- Why did I pick this up?
- Is it a healthy trait to continue, or do I need to course-correct?
- Do I like where my life is headed?

- Do I need to approach this differently?

Honest answers to these questions will tell you if you're following trends, or if you are your own man. Doing a self-assessment can give you a solid basis for following sources of influence that encourage positive traits in you.

Take control of your life. Be the man you were meant to be instead of trying to be the man rappers tell you that you should be.

CHAPTER ELEVEN

Myth #9—Affection Equals Gay

I once heard a pastor tell a story about his eight-year-old son who craved physical touch. The child loved to crawl all over his dad, enjoyed wrestling and hugs in tender moments, and often wanted to sit on his dad's lap. During the story, the pastor jokingly admitted that he wrestled with feeling gay when his son wanted to sit on his lap for extended periods of time.

We wrongly associate physical touch with romantic and sexual interest. It's become so ingrained a belief that we have a hard time deciphering physical touch in male-to-male interactions, even when it's someone like your son who obviously just loves his father and is eager to play and show his affection. Boundaries and norms within male relationships are often unclear, whether it be father to son, brother to brother, or friend to friend. Many dads feel comfortable kissing and hugging their daughters but hesitate with their sons. Many of us only understand physical affection from Mom and from a woman we desire. Obviously physical touch can be used in a sexual context, but it does not always have to be sexual.

Whether it's physical affection or words of affirmation, when it is from one man to another, there is frequently this tension and fear concerning what others might say or think. It's as if there's a hidden camera always watching to catch you in the act of showing love and somehow label you a homosexual forever. While that may sound extreme, the hoops we jump through to cover our bases are even more extreme.

For example, one of my best friends is my godbrother. We met in our teens and have been through several high highs and low lows since then. We are not related by blood, but our respective families are family. I was there with his parents and siblings when he graduated from basic training for the Navy, and I was there at the funeral of his then girlfriend who lost her life to gun violence. Years ago, we began the habit of saying, "I love you" when leaving each other's presence, especially when we knew we wouldn't see each other for an extended period of time. It was easy and natural for us, but it sometimes got awkward depending on who was listening. If there were people other than our immediate family members around, there was a hesitation to say, "I love you," because we didn't want anyone to get the wrong idea.

There's a perceived level of weakness and vulnerability that comes with affirmation and affection, so men typically don't like much attention being drawn to those moments. But let's be clear, there must be a space for a man to love another man without being in love. We know this because there's a difference between an associate and a homeboy, and there's a difference between a homeboy and a brother. We understand that there are tiers to the value we put on relationships, and that is fine to do with both women and men.

The tension of the words "I love you" being misconstrued is so strong, we commonly tag our statements with an affirmation that we're not gay, "no homo." If it's not "no homo," then it is guys in New York saying "pause." If both parties know that the other means brotherly love, why is this necessary? We are not yet comfortable caring and expressing care for another man. We put too much stock in the potential assumptions of others. While some men do grow out of this, it is still prevalent within our culture. It must be understood that it is possible—and normal—to have deep care for the life and wellbeing of another person without wanting them sexually. Additionally, we should feel free to express our love and care at any given time without looking over our shoulders to see who might be judging us and what they might be saying.

Fear of What You Don't Understand

If Dad was not there to set the tone, young men go into friendship blind and unsure of how it should look. Male relationships often don't go beyond bonding around a common interest (sports, a fraternity, work, women) or conversations that sit at the top of the communication pyramid. If you remove the common interest, you lose the relationship. If we only understand affection in a sexual or romantic context, we will fear using it elsewhere because of potential ridicule. This myth is rooted in a misunderstanding of male friendship, which I will address in the following chapter.

Interest Is Not Always Sexual

We need to understand physical affection and its purpose in straight male relationships and free ourselves from the idea that we constantly have to prove we are not gay.

If you are in a close friendship with someone that you have established over the course of several years, they understand what your sexual orientation is. There is no need to be constantly reinforcing that you prefer women over men. On a deeper level, why does care or concern for another male immediately mean homosexuality? This would assume that we only care for someone if we're interested in them sexually. Let me rephrase this important point— *we can deeply care for people outside the realm of sexuality.*

Unfortunately, the assumption that people who express care for someone are pursuing that person sexually affects how many men relate to women. Men take an interest in a woman because they believe there is a chance to engage with her sexually. However, we then transfer those troubled beliefs over to our relationships with men. Seeking to mentor black boys is difficult because a man taking an interest in another man is assumed to be rooted in some impure motive.

I've experienced that feeling in my own work. Men find it hard to believe that other men will support them and expect nothing in return.

I understand why some are hesitant—sometimes people use mentor relationships to be predatory. There is always a need to be discerning and wise in terms of who you lend your ear to and who you vent to. Be cautious. Be safe.

Staying Just Friends

One way to filter through this confusing dilemma in a healthy way is for men to have healthy female friendships that don't have an ulterior motive.

I think if you asked around, most guys may not—outside of biological sisters—have friendships with women whom they aren't trying to sleep with.

Platonic friendships will help men understand women better and themselves better. This context will expose how one can communicate on a friend level rather than a romantic level. It would benefit us all if we learned how to do this. I have many male and female friends, but I must say my female friends are the most considerate and thoughtful. Because we're not romantically involved, they relate to me as a friend or brother, and I've been able to learn from them, thus making me a better friend to my male friends. Generally speaking, I believe women may be a bit stronger in this area. However, we miss out on the opportunity to learn because we only pursue romantic relationships with women and not friendships.

Caring for someone without a motive might be a starting point in befriending a woman. Many women are adept at sensing motives, and many long for friendships such as this. It's a good start in understanding how to care for both sexes without ulterior motives.

Sexuality, the Taboo

Since we're on the topic of avoiding the appearance of being gay in our relationships with other men, I think it's important that we also address the topic of how we view gay men in our community. How we view them plays a huge part in why we fear association. Disclaimer: the following views are my own, and I do feel confident that they are right. However, today, it seems as if there are two camps—LGBTQIA people and allies and anti-LGBTQIA people. I do not fit into either camp, and I will offer critiques of both. I do not support hate or abuse of any individual based on their sexuality. I believe everyone should be treated with dignity. With that said, buckle your seatbelts.

History in the Hood

Everyone gather around. Here's where it gets real. When a man breaks a woman's heart and she is determined to get him back after the breakup, there are certain vindictive things she might say, whether they are true or not. She will either claim he has a small penis or accuse him of being gay. These two accusations will end an argument and are stigmas that no man wants attached to him. Being gay is one of the worst, if not the worst, labels for a man from the hood. Most fathers and mothers would have a harder time accepting a gay son than a gay daughter. It is looked at as an abnormal deviation from true masculinity. If you did not see that perspective in your community, you saw it in hip hop.

With the newly accepted outlook of today, many would label hip hop music of the past as very homophobic. This is the reality of where many of us come from, and it doesn't mesh well with the pro-gay majority view of today, where you can be canceled for not being supportive. I'm simply pointing out that these realities are at odds.

This becomes clear in the two or three instances where Migos members were forced to apologize for making "anti-gay" remarks. We must face the fact that many of us were raised to be anti-gay. The subject is so radioactive that actors Michael B. Jordan and Ryan Coogler came under fire online for "looking gay" in their *Vanity Fair* magazine cover in which Michael palmed Ryan's head.[12] The same thing happened with biological brothers Slim Jxmmi and Swae Lee of Rae Sremmurd with their cover for *Fader* magazine.[13] Then there's the tweets that kept Kevin Hart from hosting the Oscars. If you do not recall, he jokingly addressed what would happen if his son claimed to be gay.[14] To be honest, many of us grew up being taught that being gay is bad. That view is not necessarily changing, but public pressure and potential financial loss are causing us to tuck those views.

Gay Is Not the New Black

After years of making strides, I believe the LGBTQIA community and their activists have successfully branded their agenda alongside the civil rights movement. In a way, they have co-opted a struggle that was not their own. I do not think it's historically accurate or logically consistent to equate the fight for LGBTQIA rights with the struggle of the civil rights movement.

I say this without animosity and sheerly based on history and facts. If we look back over America's history, we see that, at one point, gay people were not allowed to marry. When we look at the black experience, historically, our personhood was questioned, and we did not have the right to vote, to learn in certain schools, to eat or drink in certain restaurants, or to take public transportation without strings attached, and we couldn't live without potentially being unjustly arrested, hosed, or attacked by dogs. Then there's slavery. This was our reality, based on our skin color, which is something we cannot hide, whereas someone could be gay and go unnoticed.

Additionally, for some, a gay lifestyle is a choice, whereas being black is not a choice for anyone. While many of the aforementioned laws have been overturned, the value of black life is still to be decided, and I say this based on inequality within our criminal justice system. All of this while the LGBTQIA community now has the power to end careers based on offensive tweets. This is just to say that the experiences are very different and should be treated as such.

The Line in the Sand

I believe my next point is a major key, but it may cause pushback and slander. I will therefore bear in mind the words of my elementary school English teacher: "Less is more."

Two things can be true at once.

Some people oppose the LGBTQIA community and their agenda with hate as their motivation. This has led and continues to lead to people saying hurtful things and committing terrible acts like physical abuse or murder. This is wrong and should be opposed.

Others can choose not to be an ally of the LGBTQIA community with faith as their motivation. For example, one basic aspect of Christianity is the idea of self-denial pertaining to anything that opposes the morality of God, including a homosexual lifestyle. The Bible presents marriage as God's idea of a covenant between a man and a woman, the two sexes He created within the creation narrative. Christians are expected to deny self and pursue what God presents as better despite how they feel.

With that said, one can choose not to support the LGBTQIA community simply because one is pursuing God's way. If someone from the LGBTQIA community has a problem with that, their issue is ultimately with God, and not necessarily His followers. Let's aim to coexist without demonizing the other side, and let's be clear that not every disagreement is rooted in hate, although some are.

Solutions to Break the Misconception

The solution to breaking the misconception that affection is exclusively feminine is to understand and have confidence in our sexuality and our friends' sexuality. We must recognize that certain kinds of affection provide encouragement and support within male relationships, too.

Open emotional expression between men is key. We get excited when a friend hits a game-winning shot. Why can't we express our happiness outside of those moments of extreme excitement? You wouldn't want to share a success with a friend who can't be excited for you because he doesn't want to express emotion. Expressing your excitement for a friend's accomplishments and happy moments doesn't translate to wanting to have sex with him. We need to have the emotional maturity to know the difference.

Breaking the stigma surrounding male-to-male affection can get weird and awkward. I think that the awkwardness is worth working through for the benefit of having healthy, substantial, deep, long-term friendships. Sometimes you will need to bounce things off other men. But if you haven't established a male friendship where you can be honest about what's going on in your relationships, careers, and emotional life, you're missing out on one of life's greatest gifts.

That's what friends are for. And having a strong male friend doesn't make you weak or less of a man. Friendships need to go beyond simply sharing a common interest, such as watching the game together or going to events to get women. Our relationships need to move beyond such a superficial level to arrive at a space where we are talking about deep things.

Expressing emotions is key. But also, the other friend receiving the information needs to not be questioned if they are taking interest in supporting a friend emotionally. We need to stop being worried about what other people think as we respond to our true friends.

Breaking the stigma surrounding affection between men will also allow us to have a healthy view of gay men, their romantic intentions, and their need for friends. A man who is secure in his sexuality should not feel the need to demean another man for his sexuality, though it may be different.

I believe it's important to point out some of our moral inconsistencies. Many of us peacefully associate with straight friends who abuse the women in their lives or who have abandoned their children. We do this while simultaneously refusing to associate with gay men. Sexuality is not a character trait. There are straight men with bad character and gay men with good character. You do not have to go find a couple of gay friends, but please consider the moral consistency in the company you keep.

CHAPTER TWELVE

Myth #10—Only Romantic Relationships Require Work

Healthy fathers produce healthy sons. Healthy sons are healthy friends. Healthy friendships create healthy fathers, and the cycle continues.

Many men accept that relationships with women require work but don't put any effort into building and maintaining friendships with men. There is a segment of men in society who think that friendships (male to male) should not require any taxing work while romantic relationships (male to female) require work because women insist on it. They believe that friendships are created and sustained organically and that women need and demand more from the other party simply because "that's just how they are."

Other guys take a very transactional approach and only maintain relationship with women they are sleeping with and men who have something to offer (finances, connections, influence, fame). These patterns can be attributed to us putting all our attention into our rotating romantic relationships while disregarding how we show up as a son, friend, and father. Additionally, many men struggle with communication. Rather than strengthening ourselves in that area, we tend to just avoid situations that require more from us.

The Reality of Relationship

Any relationship of substance is going to require work. However, working through issues with someone first requires the ability for both parties to do this individually. How I show up as a friend heavily depends on the stability or lack thereof in my personal life. If you can't understand who you are as an individual, you aren't going to be able to work well with other people. This is going to put strain on your relationships.

Knowing and understanding yourself will help you express yourself—your wants, needs, and expectations for the relationship. Whether we are aware of them or not, we all have expectations, and we often make the mistake of assuming the other party knows what they are. On a personal level, we are in conflict with ourselves at times. With that said, we should go into friendship recognizing that there is potential for conflict because we're now dealing with another imperfect person.

The Reality of Love

I'm bringing gendered relationships back up because we cannot be so fully invested in female relationships at the expense of male relationships. Many of us believe our relationships with women are the cure-all, that female liaisons are the only relationships worth having. We desire them as a place of refuge. Having a woman's attention and care isn't a bad thing, but there is no reason to only connect with women. A lack of transparent relationships with other men, that occasionally come with accountability, is a personal loss.

My next comments have been misconstrued and considered generalized by some, yet they have helped many with whom I've shared these words. Oftentimes, men run to women because they want to be coddled. It's as if they are looking for a mother to care for, understand, and pamper them. Of course, not all women coddle and enable—far from it. But many men know how to manipulate emotions.

If a man is doing something wrong or not meeting expectations, he may try to appeal to a woman's emotions in hopes of getting an emotional response rather than a stern response. Simply put, some men exhibit a pattern of expecting accountability from men and enablement from women, so they run from men to women for coddling.

You should always be wary of a man who only establishes and maintains relationships with women and doesn't maintain deep, healthy relationships with other men. A lot of times, they avoid male friendships because they are running from confrontation. They know certain aspects of their life are subpar, and a true male friend will challenge them to rise higher.

Such a confrontation, if done the right way, is a catalyst for developing healthy, substantially deep relationships between men. When I'm missing the mark or my brother is missing the mark, we can help hold each other accountable. For example, a longtime friend wanted to leave his bride early in their marriage. We both had the same mentor, and when my buddy mentioned his desire to end his marriage, the mentor issued a sharp rebuke about being self-centered and making vows to this woman yet wanting to leave because his expectations weren't being met. He added that this was selfish, and that said friend was not leading well. That was the healthy rebuke he needed, and to this day, he is grateful to that mentor. My friend and his wife are approaching twenty years of marriage.

Brotherhood, mentoring relationships, and close

friendships aren't something to run away from. They help us become better humans. We need to be surrounded by men who can challenge us and work through difficulties with us. In addition, being held accountable when we are doing something wrong and being encouraged to do things in a better way is a valuable resource.

The Reality of Friendship

I would argue that sometimes a man can be a better asset to a woman he's partnered to if he makes healthy friendships a priority. When he understands differences between people and how to communicate in both male and female friendships, he will be a better person in a dating or marriage relationship.

For example, male friendships run into trouble when one friend offends another. A lot of times, a man does not work through the issue with said friend. We internalize the offense and never deal with the problem. The thing is, it's still sitting between them, and when the next issue happens, they may still be thinking about that previous issue. The frustration of the old issue compounds the frustration of the new issue and informs how the offended party responds—usually by blowing up and saying, "This happens all the time!" We tend to exaggerate when we're offended.

When a man is offended by another man, they either go to the extreme of compartmentalizing and pretending the offense is not there and living in awkward friendship or being overly aggressive to show bravado and lack of concern for the situation. Men have a hard time admitting that another man can hurt them deeply. They don't want to reveal that they are moved by the actions of another man. However, this is normal when a relationship has been established. They think they shouldn't address the offense because:

- It is emotional/weak.

- Someone will think they are high-maintenance.

- It will run their friend off.

- Men aren't supposed to care that much anyway.

A good close friend recognizes that friendship is difficult and meaningful ones require work as seasons of life
change. People do sometimes outgrow each other, but one
friend's growth could be a healthy challenge for the other
friend to grow as well. Be willing to work through tough
issues with men if you want your groomsmen to still be
around after your wedding. Sometimes you need a
friend's ear when your marriage gets rough.

I would be suspicious of someone who can't maintain
friendships but wants to get married. Sometimes we don't
correlate marriage and friendships, but maintaining
friendships requires some of the same people skills re-
quired for marriage. As men, we don't always hold
ourselves accountable for damaged relationships we have
had in the past. We expect things to be different when we
connect to different people, but we forget that we are still
wallowing in our lack of people skills. We need to resolve
our broken relationships. And if we don't resolve them as
well as our internal issues, then we are going to carry that
baggage into the next relationship, potentially damaging
that person and that relationship as well. This is doubly
true for marriage.

Once again, these cycles can be broken if we are in a
community with other men who confront us about our issues. Whether it's challenging us to do better or dealing
with an offense, friendships are mandatory. We need to
admit that the words of the people we love matter. They

affect us, and that's why we appreciate the affirmation when we receive praise and are frustrated when they put us down. You have to accept that there are people whose words and actions affect you. Once you realize that you are vulnerable, you are in a healthy enough space to get to the point where you care for people because they are vulnerable, too.

The Reality of Brokenness

There are many guys who are damaged because of father issues, the impact of which continues throughout life. Because of this, they never take the time to get close to people. They make sure each relationship is transactional because with their father, time and relational investments were all one-way. They keep people at a distance so that other people don't have a chance to hurt them because the one person they let in, who was supposed to love them, broke them.

Negative feedback or attacks won't affect a man who doesn't prioritize how other people view him. Some guys stay in that space intentionally to protect themselves. They don't want to risk the possibility of being damaged by someone else. Once again, this is a coping mechanism that may work temporarily but doesn't benefit anyone long term, especially if they are planning on having long-term relationships with their parents, getting married, or having children.

We need to work through our standoffishness so that we can prepare our children to do better. If we don't want to be like our fathers, it's time to change. If a father has never taken the time to work through personal issues and offenses, how will he be able to maintain a relationship with his child while working through an issue with them and come to a place of forgiveness and reconciliation?

In the same way, if you don't know how to foster these

traits in yourself, then you have nothing to pass on to your kids. As I have said many times, we repeat the cycle. My children will likely be ignorant of the same things of which I am ignorant, and they will carry my baggage into their relationships. You need to do the work personally and then do the work relationally with other people. Your children will watch and do as you do.

Breaking the cycle of broken relationships begins with you. Relationships are going to be tested if they're substantial and of value. That's normal for everyone. Offenses are also normal. Difficulties are normal. Frustration is normal.

Identify the brokenness in your life so you can go into a relationship and be transparent about it. Mature and self-aware individuals can identify their own brokenness, but therapists, mentors, and family members are typically the ones to observe a pattern that reveals it.

I hate to see people lose relationships because both parties lack the ability to communicate how they were offended and work through difficult issues. So many relationships end due to a lack of communication skills. When men don't know how to communicate emotions, when we are scared to express our feelings when we're hurt, we end up losing the relationship completely. This is unfortunate, and I think there is so much more that can be done if we take the time to do the work to understand ourselves better.

A New Reality

Once again, relationships aren't meant to be about getting something. Relationships are meant to be about people supporting each other.

If I'm having an issue in my marriage, sometimes a friend will be a great support. Yes, I'm committed to my spouse for life, but sometimes a friend is there to remind me of my commitments when I'm questioning. Conversely, sometimes my spouse will be there to help me with some of the difficulties with my friends.

Don't be fully invested in one relationship and not some of the others, because no relationship is one-hundred percent perfect all the time. Sometimes another person can offer the support to keep other relationships going, but we need to have the discernment to know which relationships we should maintain and continue to work on during the tough times.

So, how do you work through offenses and hardships?

- Admit to both yourself and the other person that you were hurt rather than lying by saying, "I'm good," which many men do.

- Accept if you did the hurting, even if it was unintentional. Acknowledge the impact on the other party.

- Apologize and mean it.

- Be willing to bring in an unbiased mediator if you can't find common ground.

- Accept that you can contribute to fixing the problem even if you're the offended party.

- Offer grace and patience when working with people's issues, because you want patience with your brokenness and flaws.

- Don't bottle offenses up and then reveal them in heated moments. That is the worst time to do so.

Working through offenses, hardships, depression, and low points in relationships is worth the effort. Whether it's with your mom, dad, sister, brother, or spouse, developing relationships is vital for a fulfilling life. It starts with working on self. Once you understand yourself, you'll be able to help others and grow closer to them.

Do the work. It's worth every bit of energy you put into it.

CHAPTER THIRTEEN

Where We Go from Here

Many fathers believe the myth that their only role is to provide food and shelter. To bring everything full circle and to a close, the responsibility lies with fathers to realize that their key purpose goes beyond providing the bare necessities. Fathers are responsible for spiritual guidance, emotional shepherding, and preparing their sons to grow into men and become independent adults. This preparation includes financial stewardship, education, how to approach romantic relationships and friendships, and how to live a respectable life and leave a positive legacy. There is so much that a father is tasked with beyond providing food and shelter, and sometimes that means being the authoritarian or disciplinarian.

Fathers have neglected and, in some cases, been ill-prepared for their responsibilities for too long, and it is having a long-term effect on our young boys and men. This ideology may sound overwhelming, and it should. Fatherhood is a weighty responsibility. We need to take sex and creating children seriously while still recognizing how gratifying it can be to see our children grow into who they are once we've provided them with a firm foundation.

There is hope if we take ownership and seek discipline.

This Is for You

I recognize that I've said a lot leading up to this point. Some shoes may fit you, and some may not. Whether you identify with the good or the bad, there is always room to grow, and growth starts by taking the first step. Here are some practical ways to begin implementing what you have been presented.

For the Fathers

You may realize now that you could have done better with your son in one way or another other. This feeling is not uncommon. Many of us were not taught, so our first child ended up being another plate to balance while attempting to manage other chaotic areas of our lives. The past is the past. Don't attempt to forget it just yet, because those memories may hold significance for your son. My recommendation is to not let the past keep you from taking steps toward making a new future. Every breath is another opportunity for change.

1. You do not need to be perfect before going back to address your son. However, you must be at a point where you can communicate without being damaging to him. Often, when someone critiques us, we try to deflect their criticism by picking away at their credibility. We tear them down to invalidate what they are saying about us. It would be ideal for you to first get to a point where you can receive critical feedback without blowing up. This is essential for restoring broken or fractured relationships. Speaking as a son who was abandoned, we are forced to train ourselves to live without you. Your reappearing in itself might be a sensitive issue, so ensure that the reconnection is a beneficial one by preparing yourself first.

2. After readying yourself, approach your son with a listening ear. You may have apologies, concerns, and clarifications that you'd like to express, but it is important to first see where he is. Without having any expectations, just go back and seek to understand his feelings. This may take several meetings. Start with listening rather than speaking.

3. Whether your son raises concerns or you are already aware, take ownership and apologize for where you went wrong. Do so in a specific way. Rather than saying, "No one is perfect," say, "I am sorry for not having the discipline to be the father you deserved."

4. Accept the messiness of the process. Too often, fathers want to jump back into their sons' lives in an authoritative role. Although you have the title, you may not have the relational placement. Trust needs to be rebuilt to get back to that place. Also, recognize that your son may be inconsistent in his communication with you. He may be open and engaging one week and withdrawn the next. There is no clear-cut way to measure the impact your mistakes have had on him. Allow him the grace to figure out his new boundaries with you.

For the Sons

1. Remember that dads can be heroes, but they are still men. Too often, we rob our parents of their humanity by expecting them to do things perfectly the first time. We must remove this expectation in order to see them properly. Your dad made a mistake, or many mistakes, but this is common to all men. This does not excuse bad behavior, but it does help us to calibrate our minds in terms of our expectations. You must do the work of weighing the good and the bad and decide whether you're comfortable moving forward. If you choose to do so, be realistic. Your dad's admission of wrongdoing does not guarantee perfection moving forward. If you are blessed to be able to patch things up with your dad, know that going forward, you will experience difficulties just like you do with any other relationship.

2. I want to specifically recommend therapy to sons who have tumultuous relationships with their dads. I say this because while I've identified some of the common effects I've seen on sons, it gets even more complex than that. Mental health professionals have the skill set to dig in and see how your experience affected you. These effects can take on many different forms, even outside of what I've described in this book. You would serve yourself and your family well to know your weaknesses, potential blind spots, and insecurities.

3. Before meeting your dad, take the time to organize your thoughts and list your concerns. Many of us don't normally express how we feel. So, when raw emotion overtakes us while we're addressing our dads, we may experience word vomit. Although accusations and frustrations may freely flow out in no particular order and that may be helpful for you, it will not be helpful for your dad. It's not fair to expect a man to respond well to being shouted at and torn down. Make sure that you know what you want to say and communicate it clearly so the focus can be on what is being said rather than how it is being said. Remember the words of Mase: "Breathe, stretch, shake, let it go."

For the Man Seeking Guidance

Maybe you don't identify as a problematic father or a damaged son, but you recognize that you've been functioning under the assumption of one or more of the myths.

1. Define masculinity for yourself. In doing so, I hope that you include what I've laid out here, but even more so, I hope that you work through that definition with a trusted man who is further along in life than you. It's important to have your own definition of masculinity. Otherwise, you will constantly contort yourself as the culture shifts, thus giving others control of your life and your thinking.

I call this a masculinity detox. Whether it's hip hop, street culture, familial norms, or assumptions about what a man should be, we have accepted many things that are unhealthy and unhelpful. We must unlearn the toxic things and replace them with more nuanced views. I will go so far as to say that the masculinity many of us have adopted is, in part, what broke our families and created "baby mamas" and the single mother struggle. Additionally, be sure to include women in that defining process, as it does not serve the community to adopt ideals of manhood that appeal to men yet damage women.

2. Take a survey of your relationships. Ask the people in your life what kind of son, friend, brother, or father you are to them. Get an idea of how the people who are closest to you view you. So many of us have tunnel vision—we're so focused on a woman or women that we are blind to the fact that our other relationships are suffering. Bad sons are typically bad boyfriends. Bad friends are typically bad husbands. We tend to establish relationships, then disappear and assume the best. Be more open to relationship maintenance in all areas, which starts with asking how your loved ones feel about you.

3. Becoming a better you may require letting go of certain relationships. Some of the people you attached yourself to came along during your less-enlightened phase. You were on the same page when you met, but now that you've been enlightened, they may not fit into your life anymore. While you are moving forward, they may still be where they were when you met them. This doesn't have to end as a blow-up. Simply state your case on where you're intending to go and allow them to take a stance as well. It could go either way, and both are fine.

4. Create a new circle. By circle, I do not mean just friends but a group of people who know you, love you, and are willing to challenge you when necessary. Many men end up repeating childhood cycles in their 40s and 50s because they lack this relational dynamic. Who do you have in your life to tell you when you're trippin'? Having yes-men in your circle only stifles growth. Additionally, include people with whom you may disagree. This will help sharpen you and broaden your perspective. Once again, if everyone agrees, you may be in an echo chamber where everyone is on the same page, but you all may have the same blind spots and weaknesses.

Some of the ideas presented in this book may challenge a thought process you've held throughout your life. There are several factors that play into personal morals and worldview. I've stated where I stand on those things, and I believe my approach is generally helpful. However, your life is unique, which is why I encourage you to use this book, or a subject within a chapter, as a conversation starter. Work through the ideas presented herein with a friend or family member and see where you land.

We can learn from our mistakes, but we can also learn from the wisdom and examples of others so that we don't make the same mistakes our fathers did. Not only are you learning, but you are also going to be able to inspire and educate your future children so that they can avoid those mistakes as well. That two-fold learning from the wisdom of others and from past mistakes can inspire generational change. Even if you aren't a father, a lot of the messages here will help you be a better friend, a better son, a better brother, a better boyfriend, and a better husband.

Do you know how big this is? You can affect people in positive ways that encourage them to change for the better. Even if you are isolated, your decisions have implications for other people. By doing the work of unlearning and retraining the mind, I believe you can move forward with the wisdom that you gain and make a positive difference in the lives of those to whom you are connected.

Men are at different points in life. Some are just stepping into manhood. Some have been enjoying manhood for years. Hopefully at any point in time, wherever you are in life, my words here can both challenge you to identify your personal need for change as well as inspire you to have the courage to pursue it.

CONCLUSION

Whole Brother Mission

You could be a young guy, an old head, or even a single mom reading this, and you want help. The contents of this book may be triggering for some. It is very hard to deal with deep wounds and unresolved family issues. This book may start the conversation, but what's next? I did not want to add to the constant criticism that black men and people receive without actively being a part of the solution. This is why, after addressing each myth, I've attempted to offer a better way. Additionally, I want to be able to offer a personalized experience of support for you. The concerns raised here are what inspired me to launch the Whole Brother Mission, a 501(c)(3) nonprofit corporation that seeks to equip men to be whole in every area of life by focusing on our three core areas:

The head (Mental Health). We connect under-resourced male clients to licensed mental health professionals (counselors, therapists, psychiatrists).

The heart (Emotional Maturity). Some hesitate to visit a medical or mental health professional, so we also connect our clients with life coaches and mentors for additional support at no charge.

The hands (Professional Advancement). We offer an

online life skills program with several different courses covering financial literacy, entrepreneurship, and higher education.

Stability in these three areas will not ensure a smooth life, but it will provide a firm foundation. If you or someone you know may be in need of these services, please connect with us via our website, www.wholebrothermission.com. Our work is made possible through charitable giving. If you or someone you know has a passion for mental health advocacy, the black community, or support services for men, please direct them to our website as well for ways to connect for volunteer work or to support our work financially. All gifts are tax deductible. Spread the word! Thank you for reading!

About the Author

Originally from Southeast Washington, D.C., Maliek now resides in Southern California, where he serves as the CEO of the Whole Brother Mission—a nonprofit that seeks to equip men to be whole in every area of life. The Whole Brother Mission accomplishes this by providing its members with assisted access to licensed professional counseling/therapy, mentorship, and an online life skills program that centers on entrepreneurship, higher education, and financial literacy. Before joining the Whole Brother Mission, Maliek worked as a university dean and a diversity consultant. He is completing a doctoral degree in counseling, and his focus is facilitating conversations that challenge the public to analyze their views on family, friendship, and identity.

REFERENCES

Notes

¹ Jensen, Shelley, dir. *The Fresh Prince of Bel-Air*. Season 4, episode 24, "Papa's Got a Brand New Excuse." Aired May 9, 1994, on NBC. In "Quotes." *The Fresh Prince of Bel Air: Papa's Got a Brand New Excuse.* IMDB. https://www.imdb.com/title/tt00583018/quotes/?tab=qt&ref_= tt_trv_qu.

² Loritts, Bryan. *Insider Outsider: My Journey as a Stranger in White Evangelicalism and My Hope for Us All.* Zondervan, 2018.

³ Donne, John. "Meditation XVII: No Man Is an Island." In *Devotions Upon Emergent Occasions.* W. Pickering, 1840.

⁴ Chapman, Gary. *The Five Love Languages.* Northfield Publishing, 2010.

⁵ Naqi, Kelly. "In Virginia Facing State Dogfighting Charges, Vick's Involvement Revealed." ESPN. November 21, 2008.

https://www.espn.com/nfl/news/story?id=3718304.

[6] Henderson, Cydney. "Terry Crews Settles Lawsuit with the Hollywood Agent He Says Groped Him." USA Today. September 6, 2018. https://www.usatoday.com/story/life/ people/2018/09/06/terry-crews-settles-lawsuit-hollywood- agent-he-says-groped-him/1216837002/.

[7] Breakfast Club Power 105.1 FM. "DeVon Franklin on 'The Truth About Men', Mastering the Dog, Love Vs. Lust + More." YouTube video. https://www.youtube.com/watch?v= TFyMLXRtjfI.

[8] Breakfast Club Power 105.1 FM, "DeVon Franklin on 'The Truth About Men.'"

[9] God, Charlamagne Tha. *Shook One: Anxiety Playing Tricks on Me.* Atria Books, 2019.

[10] Lil Wayne. "Pussy, Money, Weed." Track 13 on Michael Watts, *Final Chapter 2K7 Chopped and Screwed.* Swishahouse (BCD Music Group), 2008.

[11] McCurley, Ione. "Lil Wayne Says He Was Raped at Age 11." The Urban Daily. November 20, 2009. https://theurbandaily.com/437467/lil-wayne-says-he-was- raped-at-age-11/.

[12] "This Michael B. Jordan Photo in Vanity Fair Has People Upset—Here's Why." Yahoo! Lifestyle. March 7, 2016. https://www.yahoo.com/lifestyle/michael-b-jordan-photo- vanity-180700543.html.

[13] Zeichner, Naomi. "Rae Sremmurd's Best Life." *Fader.* Vol.

104, Summer 2016. https://www.thefader.com/2016/06/07/ rae-sremmurd-sremmlife-2-cover-story-interview.

[14] Holcombe, Madeline and Joe Sutton. "Kevin Hart Says He Won't Host Oscars After Furor Over Homophobic Tweets." CNN. December 7, 2018. https://www.cnn.com/2018/12/07/ entertainment/kevin-hart-oscars-step-down/index.html.

Made in the USA
Monee, IL
22 May 2020

31560986R00075